M000082879

Dragons
For Beginners

About the Author

Shawn MacKenzie (North Bennington, VT) had her first Dragon encounter when she was four years old, when she happened upon an a copy of *The Dragon Green* by J. Bissell-Thomas. A sci-fi/fantasy writer, she is an avid student of myth, religion, philosophy, and animals real, imaginary, large, and small.

To Write to the Author

If you wish to contact the author or would like more information about this book, please write to the author in care of Llewellyn Worldwide, and we will forward your request. Both the author and publisher appreciate hearing from you and learning of your enjoyment of this book and how it has helped you. Llewellyn Worldwide cannot guarantee that every letter written to the author can be answered, but all will be forwarded. Please write to:

Shawn MacKenzie
℅ Llewellyn Worldwide
2143 Wooddale Drive
Woodbury, MN 55125-2989

Please enclose a self-addressed stamped envelope for reply, or $1.00 to cover costs. If outside the USA, enclose an international postal reply coupon.

Dragons

For Beginners

Ancient Creatures in a Modern World

SHAWN MACKENZIE

Llewellyn Publications
Woodbury, Minnesota

FIRST EDITION
Second Printing, 2018

Book format by Bob Gaul
Cover art: Dragon © Linda Bucklin/Shutterstock.com
Cover design by Adrienne Zimiga
Editing by Nicole Nugent

Llewellyn Publications is a registered trademark of Llewellyn Worldwide Ltd.

Library of Congress Cataloging-in-Publication Data
MacKenzie, Shawn, 1954–
  Dragons for beginners: ancient creatures in a modern world/by Shawn MacKenzie.
     p. cm.
  ISBN 978-0-7387-3045-5
1. Dragons. I. Title.
  GR830.D7M344 2012
  398.24'54—dc23
                          2012012037

Llewellyn Worldwide Ltd. does not participate in, endorse, or have any authority or responsibility concerning private business transactions between our authors and the public.
  All mail addressed to the author is forwarded, but the publisher cannot, unless specifically instructed by the author, give out an address or phone number.
  Any Internet references contained in this work are current at publication time, but the publisher cannot guarantee that a specific location will continue to be maintained. Please refer to the publisher's website for links to authors' websites and other sources.

Llewellyn Publications
A Division of Llewellyn Worldwide Ltd.
2143 Wooddale Drive
Woodbury, MN 55125-2989
www.llewellyn.com

Printed in the United States of America

Other books by Shawn MacKenzie

The Dragon Keeper's Handbook

contents

part II: Dragons in Faith, Magic, and the Arts

part III: Living with Dragons

epilogue: Pondering the Unthinkable: A World Without Dragons 225

For my father,
who taught me to see with wonder.

Acknowledgments

Special thanks to my fellow writers on both sides of North Branch. With patience, fresh eyes, and open minds, they followed me into Dragon Country and kept me on track when I was tempted to stray.

In the beginning,
The Great Cosmic Dragon kissed the sun.
Her fiery wings held close the earth.
The air shook with Her thunderous smile.

—Shawn MacKenzie

Welcome to Dragon Country

Somewhere between the craggy mountains of modern science and the forested lowlands of primordial myth, thunder rolls across lapis skies and the air is fragrant with spice and fire.

This is Dragon Country.

It's a land I've known since I was no more than knee-high to a kickle snifter. Through the years I have explored it, cardinal point to point, growing gray among its residents. I have gone Dragon-watching from Europe to the Pacific Northwest, from desert sands to glacial floes. I've seen enchantments bathe in Iceland's thermal pools and tail-dance along Vermont's Green Mountains.

Ah, I sense a whiff of incredulity in the air. "Dragons? You've seen Dragons?"

The poet Ralph Hodgson was fond of saying, "Some things have to be believed to be seen." In the realm of weyr (Dragon community) and wing, this is as close to gospel as it gets. And why shouldn't we believe? From prehistory to the present, Dragons have informed our species' ties with a mix of wonder, skepticism, dread, and—ultimately—mighty leaps of faith. Of course, being open to the rare and unusual and to the hidden all around us is a subjective thing, even more so when it comes to beings who sail the eternal winds between reality and myth. That said, the range and power of Dragons is such that they have fared far better than a host of lesser creatures, capturing the imagination so that, whether we love them or loathe them, even when out of sight, Dragons are never out of mind.

Personally, I prefer to love them.

My first Dragon sighting occurred in 1963, in Devonshire, England, on the rural fringes of Dartmoor. Prime Dragon Country. Moor and woodland, the wilderness was a playground for me! One particular haunt of mine was a dense beech and rhododendron forest surrounding a deserted mica mine, which I explored whenever I could. On one such trek, out of the corner of my eye, I spied something—something large—quietly weaving in and out of the woods. I turned, but there was nothing there. A play of my imagination, I figured, continuing on my way. Then I saw it again—on the other side of the lane! I stopped and stared hard, trying to pick out a creature from the camouflaging bands of shade and filtered sun. Something had moved, I was sure of it.

Suddenly, with a roar and a whoosh that knocked me flat, a young emerald green Dragon flew out of the woods, swooped over my head, circled the mine, then zoomed straight up through the canopy and disappeared.

I was dumbstruck. Not scared, just … wowed! Even in England, I knew you didn't see Dragons every day. Yet I had. For some reason, the Great Dragon had smiled on me that day, and blessed me with my first real live Dragon encounter.

Of course, how we think of Dragons has a lot to do with our initial contacts. The first Dragons I met all those years ago were not frightful monsters but fiercely loyal guardians against the terrors of the dark. Over the decades, they changed as I did. They became larger, more intelligent, and more complex. More wild. Striving to keep up, to be the best Dragon person I could, and to understand them as best I could, I threw myself into their history and ways, both natural and mystical. I discovered tales and wonders along the way, and all sorts of Dragons. They never asked much, never demanded parades or unconditional approval (though we've given them the former and, as for the latter, well, anyone who's spent an afternoon around a weyr knows we're none of us perfect). No, they simply wanted to be seen in all their elaborate, sometimes-messy truth—from horned brow to spiky tail—and respected for the beings they are, like every other traveler on the planet.

From respect comes appreciation; from appreciation, love. What could be simpler?

Unfortunately, I discovered there is little simple about our long history with Dragons. A lot of bad blood lingers on both sides. For our part, it's further complicated by fictions, superstitions, and outright lies, tumbling headlong into blind disbelief. In the face of all that, there is only one answer: the truth. In Wales, land of many Dragons, there is a saying: *Y gwir yn erbyn y bydd!* "Truth against the world!" And nothing imparts truth like a tête-à-tête with a Dragon. It is an experience guaranteed to beat back the darkest night like Dragonfire, and to remind us that, across leagues and eons, Dragons remain the one universal, familiar bit of magic we carry with us. And in return they carry our awe. Surely theirs is the weightier burden!

For that reason alone, these great ancient creatures are as necessary today as they ever were. And yet there is so much more to love about Dragons. They teach us to keep connected with the planet, which is critical these days when Earth's delicate balance is in danger of being shattered. The more we lose touch with the wilderness and the damage we've done to the world, the more we need Dragons to remind us of our place in the natural order of things and the responsibility we owe to each other and to the planet. By consorting with Dragons we are able to tap into the better parts of ourselves, to be inspired by their courage, loyalty, justice, and family devotion. Even their humility—yes, Dragons can be humble—can teach us. The study of Dragons is little less than the study of the world: zoology, biology, physics, chemistry, toxicology, aeronautics, mythology, cosmology, religion, ontology, ethics, sociology, even Dragon lore ... the list goes on and on, in short, encompassing what it means to be human.

We need to keep Dragons in the modern world so that we might keep the mystery and wonder in our lives. We ignore Dragons at our own—and the world's—peril.

For those of you new to the world of Dragons, let this book be your guide. In Part I, you will be introduced to the basic scientific facts—from size to diet, habitat to habits—of the three species of True Dragons: Eastern (Asian), Western (European), and Feathered (Southern or New World). You will also meet a cross section of lesser or pseudo-dragons. They are the vaguely dragonish creatures from around the world who flesh out local Dragon lore and keep Dragon-watchers on their toes. This is Dragon Studies 101, sure to guarantee that you're safe in the wild and don't make a fool of yourself at the next Dragon convention. Don't forget to consult the glossary and bibliography as needed!

Part II looks at our changing relationship with Dragons throughout history, focusing on religion, the occult sciences, and art and literature. It traces their cultural influence from their honored days in ancient China, where they influenced Taosim and the divining art of the *I Ching,* to the pages of modern faërie tales and literary fantasy; from their role as the devil's minions to their being used piecemeal for alchemists' elixirs.

Finally, in Part III, you will learn how to live with Dragons in both wild and domestic settings. You will be introduced to the rules and ways of modern Dragon sanctuaries and lay-bys as well as the fundamentals of Dragon keeping—should you be so lucky and inclined—from hatching fire to the thrill of flight and the demands and responsibilities of advanced age.

Dragons and Dragon keepers, old friends, new colleagues, comrades of scale and burning blood—I offer you these pages. They are my invitation. Come. Walk with me through Dragon Country.

Part I

Dragon Basics:
What They Are and
Why We Need Them

one

Facts, Figures, and Defining Terms

Three hundred thousand years ago, when Homo sapiens walked out of Africa, Dragons were everywhere. Around every river bend, on every mountain top, they basked at ease, the reigning predators in a wild and woolly world. Our ancient ancestors cast their eyes to the heavens and were wowed by the sheer otherworldly grandeur winging across the horizon. To primitive minds Dragons were nothing short of divine. They were the roar of sea and the blinding flash of lightning; gentle life-giving rains and inexplicable death in the night. They were the terrible danger lurking beyond the glow of village fires and the benevolent warmth of the fires themselves. Bigger, fiercer, more incredible than any other creature real or imagined, no beings—

including man—have roamed so far or evolved so well. From the dawn of time, these were Dragons. They still are.

Don't be so surprised.

Earth has managed to spawn a stellar array of life. From microscopic viruses to macroscopic pteradons, from bear cats to short-nosed bats, blue skimmers to blue whales, sporting fur, feathers, skin, and scales, the planet's biodiversity is truly spectacular. Just walk through the woods with ears pricked and eyes wide and you will find creatures, great and small, extraordinary enough to fill even the most jaded city slicker with awe. Spanning the taxonomic continuum, the common and the rare are there for the observing.

Harder to see are the mystical and the fabulous, the beings we've come to consider truly otherworldly. Griffins, unicorns, dryads, phoenix—their numbers are legion, their names and forms as varied as local habitat and custom allow. Over time many have gone the way of the moa and mammoth, a way currently slick with whale oil and strewn with tiger pelts and lyrebird quills. Those mystical creatures that remain slip in and out of the shadows, struggling to survive as environs and belief grow increasingly short in supply. They dance along the margins of medieval manuscripts and through the peripheral vision of cryptozoologists, mythologists, and literary fantasists. Thanks to a dwindling familiarity with the arcane, many incredible creatures pass without so much as a second look from humans who wouldn't know a kitsune (fox spirit) from a chipmunk. They wear the cloak of modest anonymity that allows them to avoid the dangerously acquisitive and fearfully ignorant. To linger among us a little longer.

And then there are Dragons.

Magnificent, preternatural, take-your-breath-away Dragons.

Soaring on the four winds, surfing the seven seas, Dragons have never indulged in anonymity. Tossing all notions of "local" onto the dung heap, they went global in a big way. They carved out niches in every ecosystem: burning deserts and glacial peaks, verdant tropics and scrub-grassed plains. They lashed the clouds with Dragonfire and bent low the trees with Dragonsong.

Woven into the tapestry of the Homo sapien experience, Dragons are so integral to human faith, history, science, and fiction that everyone today knows—or at least thinks they know—all about them. Yet, as eternally ubiquitous as Dragons are, our presumed knowledge of them is informed as much by individual customs, encounters, and locales as by scientific facts. While this variety is spectacular in the abstract, in practice it mixes a little truth with a lot of abject fantasy in a stew that leaves the casual Dragon aficionado confused and misinformed. If you are hoping to establish any sort of personal relationship with Dragons, this is hardly the best way to begin. In the enduring words of Mark Twain, "It ain't what you don't know that gets you into trouble. It's what you know for sure that just ain't so." When it comes to Dragons, such an approach will not only get you into trouble, it might get you killed.

Thus, as we step into the headwaters of Dragon Studies, it is important to be on the same page with respect to the basic facts, figures, and terms. To learn one's draconic ABCs.

Welcome to the world of cryptoherpetology.

"What?" you ask.

Cryptoherpetology is the branch of natural and meta-physical sciences dealing with hidden or mystical (*crypto*) reptiles and amphibians (*herpetology*). The more whimsical in the field—and lovers of alliteration—refer to it as Secret Serpent Science. Briefly put, it's Dragon Studies. Included in Dragon Studies are all Dragons—True and pseudo—as well as a collection of creatures outside simple zoological classification that tend to have one or more herpetological characteristics, most often scales. (With the exception of the fire salamander, crypto-amphibians are more faërie tale than fact and are thus irrelevant to the study at hand.)

While science is at the heart of cryptoherpetology, the field, like its subjects, is considerably more far-reaching and inclusive, spreading its branches like a great banyan tree over humanity and her cultures. Magic, religion, art, sociology—all are impacted by the study of Dragons.

A word of caution: Dragon lore is the twig on the cryptoherpetological tree that, while charming in its own way, is overburdened with fiction and shoddy scholarship—some might even call it willful deception. As a body of "information," lore clearly points to the difference between what *is* true about Dragons and what people choose to *believe* is true. For when Dragons were adopted by various cultures, their attributes were adapted to the particular needs and attitudes of the society in question. This makes for good storytelling but bad science. Any serious dracophile will temper their appreciation of lore with liberal doses of hard facts.

Those—and there are many—who would dismiss the entire field as fantasy would do well to remember the words of the noted British chemist, Sir Cyril Hinshelwood (1897–1967): "[All science is] an imaginative adventure of the mind seeking truth in a world of mystery." If that doesn't cover Dragons, nothing does.

But how does a cryptoherpetologist direct her passion? What *is* a Dragon?

The Oxford English Dictionary—gold standard for all things Anglo-lexical—takes the word back to its Greek roots: *drakōn*—"strong one"—and *derkesthai* —"to see clearly."[1] It goes on to define a Dragon as:

> *A mythical monster, represented as a huge and ter-*
> *rible reptile, usually combining ophidian and crocodil-*
> *ian structure, with strong claws, like a beast or bird of*
> *prey, and a scaly skin; it is generally represented with*
> *wings, and sometimes as breathing out fire. The heraldic*
> *dragon combines reptilian and mammalian form with*
> *the addition of wings.*

Though rather Eurocentric, this thumbnail sketch hits enough of the highlights to guarantee even the most Draco-illiterate individual can distinguish a Welsh Red from a golden retriever, though not much more. This is your standard big-*D*, or True, Dragon: large, scaly, and with a voracious appetite. This image is so rooted in our human memories that in virtually all six-thousand-plus languages of this world—and a few out of it—you can say "Dragon" and be confident you are speaking of a creature that loses little in translation. While the details might vary from region to region, the basics—particularly with reference to Western and Eastern True Dragons—

---

1. In Webster's slightly more accessible—and easier on the eyes—lexicon, *drakōn* and *derkesthai* lead back to "the seeing one," aka the Watcher. This is particularly relevant when examining Dragons as guardians and hoarders. See chapter 3.

remain essentially the same. (The third of the True Dragon species, the Feathered Dragons, are so rare that many even in the cryptozoological community almost consider them in a class by themselves. See chapter 4.)

Of course, as any dracophile will tell you, a few lines in the dictionary, no matter how well-intentioned, cannot begin to capture a fraction of all that is *Dragon*. Evidence from medieval anecdotes and natural histories (aka bestiaries), for example, argues that *dragon* was originally shorthand for any creature frightening, vaguely reptilian, and unexplained. As humankind evolved and became less afraid of the dark, we sifted through generic terrors and distilled Dragons down into the specific creatures with scales, wings, and scorching breath we know today.

Along the way, a trail of small-*d* pseudo-dragons was left running though every nook, cranny, and cultural hollow of the world. From Tierra del Fuego to the Arctic Circle, from the jungles of Asia to the Great Plains, land and sea are thick with creatures who fall under the broad draconic rubric (some of whom we will examine in chapter 5). Fascinating though they are, most are no more Dragons than puppies are whales. Still, their presence speaks to the scope of Dragons and Dragon lore, and their tales pad cryptozoology texts the world over.

More on point to our study are the issues raised by such a definition's use of the dreaded *M* words: *monster* and *mythical*. Throwing the label "monster" around is something to which many Dragon lovers—and likely most Dragons—take exception. It is a sign of human arrogance that we tag anything strange, massive, predatory—anything we don't understand—with pejoratives like "monster" or "beast," words that are reserved for the most heinous of our own kind. Thanks to Genesis, even *reptilian* is slanderous in most human circles, implying someone is mean, base, and sneaky. Though the reference speaks to our innate need for this dark element in the world, surely Dragons deserve better. Those of you who are justly offended by such name-calling can be heartened by the fact that the Latin for monster, *monstum*, can also mean "miracle" and "omen." Dragon as miracle has a nice ring to it.

Monsters or not, referring to Dragons as "mythical" clearly illustrates the limitations of conventional wisdom, even among the learned wordsmiths of the OED. Not that we should be surprised. Since Dragons are seldom seen sauntering across Oxford's ley lines or frolicking in the university's South Park duck pond, it is understandable that they are cloaked in the mantle of the fantastic. Even experts are divided on the matter, insisting Dragons are either fact, fiction, or long-ago-fact/now-extinct-fiction. This debate could take up volumes, so, for the purpose of these pages, stretch your minds and sink your mental fangs firmly into the belief that Dragons not only existed in millennia past but grace the world to this day.

True Dragons: Fundamental Facts and Shared Traits

Three species of big-*D* True Dragons claim Earth as their home: the Eastern or Oriental, the Western or Occidental, and the Feathered or Southern. Some scholars, for the sake of global continuity, include the Rainbow Serpents of Africa and Australia among the True Dragons. The consensus in the draconic community is that this works on a cosmological level but not a practical one, since modern Rainbow Serpents have only spiritual, not physical, mass. (Still, when it comes to talking Cosmic Dragons, Rainbow Serpents are up there with the best of them. See chapter 6.)

Though there are species-specific differences among this draconic trinity, there are also a few constants. All True Dragons are elemental in nature. More than any other creatures, they are connected to the Earth, their massive bodies rolling like hills, their claws digging deep like tap roots, their fiery sighs steaming like Yellowstone geysers. This relationship to the planet is believed to have played a crucial role in draconic evolution. Depending on whom you talk to, the first Dragon ancestors showed up somewhere between 250 million and 100 million years ago. Through cunning, luck, and intricate links to the planet's energy, small proto-Dragons (unrecognizable by modern standards) managed to survive extinction-level events that wiped out larger, swifter, more dominant species. They drifted with the continents to every corner of the world and, by approximately 60 million years ago, evolved into the elegant True Dragons we know today. More rigid voices in the scientific community are eager to point out that much of this is pure, though educated, conjecture. The fossil record for Dragons is all but nonexistent, which in and of itself proves nothing: fossils have only been found for a mere fraction of all species that ever existed. But it gives ammunition to those who insist that Dragons are new on the planetary scene, following the human wake rather than us following theirs.

Whether you believe Dragons are old or *very* old, the fact remains that they never lost their ties to the Earth. As people have retreated farther and farther from the natural state, Dragons remain an essential touchstone, keeping us connected with the wilder world around us—the world upon which we all must rely.

But do not confuse *wild* with *simple*. Dragons are anything but. True Dragons are social beings, not only treasuring the company of their kind but recognizing that there is strength in numbers. They live in communities known as weyrs (rhymes with *fears*). Each weyr is made up of between two and four Dragon clans or *enchantments*. In the past, before people ran rampant and land-greedy across the continents, weyrs were much larger, sheltering up to ten enchantments at a time. This led to a robust gene pool and generations of Dragons who could take on anything the world threw their way. The extended family units also provide a nurturing environment in which a mating pair—Queen and Sire—can raise their wee Dragonlets, confident they are getting the best possible start in life.

The complexity of Dragon species is also evident in their diet. True Dragons are omnivores. In fact, they will eat most anything except other Dragons. They also shy away from ingesting other reptiles, considering it bad form to dine on a cousin, no matter how distant—and modern mundane reptiles are about as far from Dragons as you can get and still have scales. That said, should push come to shove and food be scarce, all bets are off. The role vegetation plays in draconic fare is, naturally, habitat specific: the greater the abundance and diversity, the greater the consumption. A European Schwartzwald Singlehorn, for example, will have a lot more greens cross her palate than a Sahel Dunehopper from the deserts of North Africa. Zoologists are discovering that the more intricate the diet, the more intelligent the creature, and Dragons are easily the most keen-witted of the crypto species. They can even give us poor humans a run for our money.

Misunderstandings, Untruths, and Outright Lies

There is a slew of information out there about Dragons which, despite its repetition in fantasy and bestiary, is just flat-out wrong.

Dragons are not immortal. However, they are extremely long-lived. Barring accident, natural disaster, and/or human predation, it is presumed—though still unproved—that a Dragon can live to see her five hundredth birthday. This may seem immortal to us, but that view is relativistic rather than factual.

Dragons are not related to dinosaurs. This is an error in the record arising from the fact that the ancient Chinese believed great finds of dinosaur fossils were really Dragon bones, a mistake not corrected until the nineteenth century. Though their distant ancestors were around when the "terrible lizards" reigned, Dragons come from a very different branch of the evolutionary tree. Some might say it's a whole new tree altogether.

True Dragons are not strictly reptilian. Most notably, Dragons are not ectothermic (cold-blooded); nor are they endothermic (warm-blooded). They are, in fact, a little of both with a touch of gigantothermy thrown in for good measure. This means that, like megafauna—and, yes, certain dinosaurs—they rely on their considerable bulk to auto-regulate their body temperature and remain active without giving a thought to recharging their solar selves. Cold-climate Dragons have even been known to employ kleptothermy—the "stealing" or sharing of body warmth—to get themselves through long winter nights.

Unlike other reptiles, Dragons can also sport fur and feathers. But they are all scaled to one degree or another. Feathered Dragons, as their name attests, are arrayed with exquisite plumage, and the manes and ankle tufts of Oriental Dragons are legendary. Even Western Dragons emerge from their eggs with a fine fuzzy coat which serves to keep the hatchlings warm and toasty. While the majority of Western Dragons shed this infant down by the summer of their third year, rimed Siberian and Polar Dragons have been known to retain this extra layer of insulation around neck and chest well into adulthood, even letting it grow thick and shaggy. Against the biting winds and blizzarding snows, every little bit helps.

Not all True Dragons fly. And some Dragons who do fly—like the more exalted Oriental breeds—manage without benefit of wings. Scientists are still trying to figure that one out, though many simply shrug their shoulders and file it under "mysterious Dragon stuff." The fact is, as cutting-edge as cryptoherpetology is, what we don't know far outweighs what we do. At present, there are still many things about Dragons that are met with a wink, a nod, and an "Oy vey!" or "That's funny." In short, there is a lot left to discover, and the field is wide open for the curious and diligent (no slackers need apply).

Not all Dragons breathe fire. Fire is the defensive weapon of choice for Western Dragons and a select group of pseudo-dragons, like the fire drake (the name "fire drake" is a dead giveaway). Feathered Dragons are equipped with retractable fangs and huge venom glands, which they employ to lethal effect when they must, and Oriental Dragons use various mixtures of mist and venom. Western Frost Dragons, though able to breathe fire, usually opt for a less fatal approach, combining fire with ice and exhaling directed clouds of hoarfrost. This will stop any foe as fast as Medusa's stare, though less permanently. Sound is also part of the draconic defensive arsenal. A good bellow can knock birds from the sky—an unfortunate side effect—and humans off their feet. More than a few poachers have come out of Dragon Country deaf as well as empty handed.

Dragons are not nocturnal. This is a longstanding misconception popularized during the Middle Ages, when Dragons were frequently spotted lighting the night sky with their fire. The sight would have been dramatic enough to inspire the least imaginative mind—and Dragons do enjoy the dramatic. By Elizabethan times, William Shakespeare (1564–1616) had slipped the notion of these night fliers into the literary as well as the popular imagination:

> *Puck: My fairy lord, this must be done with haste,*
> *For night's swift dragons cut the clouds full fast.*
> —*A Midsummer Night's Dream* III.ii.378–79

> *Iachimo: … Swift, swift, you dragons of the night,*
> *that dawning*
> *May bare the raven's eye.*
> —*Cymbeline* II.ii.48

Some have argued that the Bard was referring not to real Dragons but to meteors streaking across the sky. While this is possible, the idea of Dragons being synonymous with shooting stars surely came from seeing Dragons reveling aloft after hours. Amateur dracophiles continued to believe Dragons were creatures of the night well into the twentieth century thanks to the dangers of the post-Industrial world that forced our friends to fine-tune their daytime camouflage. It's not that they weren't out and about during the day, they simply weren't seen. While Dragons enjoy late night romps, as far as their daily routines go, they are primarily crepuscular. This means they are active at dawn and dusk, when they can use the shifting light to shield them from view of prey and foe. Long hours of bright, tropical sun force Feathered Dragons to be the most diurnal—or daytime-active—of the big three species, hunting through their sun-drenched habitats with grace, their exceptional eyesight letting them spy a meal even through dense rain forest canopies.

A note of warning: Though dusky hours are considered best for Dragon watching, do be careful. Dragons on the wing at that time are usually hunting. As good as their vision is, half-light leads them to hunt by sound and scent as well as sight. Though they'd prefer a deer to a human, mistakes can be made even by the most scrupulous Dragon.

Dragons are not evil. The most insidious bit of misinformation about Dragons is that they are nasty, damsel-stealing, human-eating creatures. Let's break this down. First, there is no good and evil in nature. There is order and chaos, danger and innocence, balance and imbalance. Dragons, being as natural as they come, are at times chaotic or fiercely dangerous, but they are no more evil than the mouse who raids the granary or the cat who dines on that corn-fattened rodent.

As for flying off with fair maids for a late-night snack, this too is utter nonsense concocted by land-hungry chieftains looking to appropriate prime real estate occupied by local enchantments. How better to work one's minions into a fury than by terrorizing them with fears of daughters lost to ravening maws? Unfortunately, young women (wenches and princesses alike) were left as sacrificial offerings, and many of them died. But it was much more likely they succumbed to exposure or wildcat attacks than a rampant case of draconic munchies. The truth is, Dragons find us decidedly unappetizing and, given a choice, will much prefer mutton to man every day of the week. While this doesn't take humans completely off the menu, we are morsels of last resort or opportunity, as in the case of famine or Dragon hunters in the wrong place at the wrong time. Remember, Dragons will defend themselves with lethal force if need be. This is their right as creatures of the universe. Should a nosh of errant knight fall into their paws as a consequence, it will not go to waste.

Recent studies have found that the vast majority of reports of "Dragon Eats Man" should be attributed to large pseudo-dragons (wyverns, hydras, even some lake species) that find themselves at odds with the modern world. Pseudo-dragons are more consistently carnivorous and some, like the wyvern and hydra, require a lot of flesh to satisfy their appetites. As with so many other animals, we have stolen their habitat, plundered their food sources, and set many of them squarely in poachers' sights, all of which send their survival instincts into overdrive and stress their less-than-genteel natures. Naturally. Even the most harmless looking house dragon can turn killer when cornered. At the very least, they become unpredictable and righteously aggressive. Over the years, our treatment of these wonderful creatures, combined with their dining preferences, has resulted in far more humans falling prey to pseudo-dragons than True Dragons. Unfortunately, the distinction is lost on the press, who, rather than doing their homework, simply paint all draconic beings with the same bloody brush.

If your interest is piqued and you want to take that first step and venture into the world of casual Dragon watching, two simple bits of advice:

1. Work with a pro—someone who is not only used to Dragons, but who knows the environment and its inhabitants. This is advisable for anyone out among wild creatures, but even more so when the possibility of injury and even death is not exaggeration but real.

2. When in doubt about anything—species, mating cycle, the phase of the moon, *anything!*—keep your distance. A good long one. There are far too many unknowns to simply charge recklessly on, sustained only by honorable intentions and whispered prayers. Remember that all Dragons, True and pseudo, are endangered. You're in their space where their rights and lives are protected. If something nasty happens, under the law the fault is yours.

two

Oriental Dragons

Long ago, in a world of mountains newly risen and saber-sharp and crystal waters flowing from glacier to sea, sinuous, whiskered Dragons roamed the Orient from the Pacific Rim to the Central Steppes. They dined on bamboo and banyan fruit, catfish, aurochs, and pink-tusked pachyderms. And, dancing across the Gobi Desert, they kicked up dust clouds so thick they blotted out the sun from the Himalayan foothills to Siberia's Sea of Okhotsk. These were the great Eastern Dragons, forces of nature, guardians of the Earth, rulers of the rain, and gifters of good fortune.

Venerated by the civilizations that flourished in their company, these majestic creatures were once plentiful and as varied as the continent they called home. Regretfully, this is no longer so. Crossing paths with an Eastern, or Oriental, Dragon is one of the rarest blessings in the world. Centuries of tumultuous politics and severe loss of habitat have driven wild weyrs out of their once-pristine, now-urbanized lowlands and into inhospitably remote regions. This is a tragic state of affairs not only for the Dragons, but for those of us who would study and protect them. In fact, for much of the twentieth century, field research in China, Japan, and Korea was virtually unheard of.

Today, Chinese Dragons are almost never seen beyond the republic's borders—giant pandas are veritable globetrotters by comparison—and access to mainland weyrs is near impossible. All but the most privileged cryptoherpetologists must rely on lore and legend rather than firsthand information. Since many believe that all Oriental Dragons came from Chinese stock, such restrictions seriously hamper ongoing scientific studies. Still, in the name of preservation, we make do as best we can. It is delightfully humbling to remember that Dragons do not recognize borders or governmental fiats. Observant travelers—especially those in southwestern China and the Himalayan uplands—have been known to catch sight of a Dragon or two wandering far from their established sanctuaries.

Natural History: Evolution, Morphology, and Temperament

Though Oriental Dragons remain scientifically enigmatic, they are culturally familiar. For thousands of years, they have guarded temple and palace and cavorted across silk, paper, and skin. This widespread presence leads dracophiles the world over to believe they could recognize an Eastern Dragon on any crosswalk in the five continents. Thanks to oral, written, and artistic records, they are probably right. As Japanese scholar Okakura Kakuzo noted: "He is the spirit of change ... the great mystery itself ... [He] reveals himself only to vanish ... Coiling again and again on his strength, he sheds his crusted skin amid the battle of elements, and for an instant stands half revealed by the brilliant shimmer of his scales. He strikes not till his throat is touched. Then woe to him who dallies with the terrible one!"[2]

According to art and lore, your typical Oriental Dragon is serpentine, short-legged, and three- to five-toed (depending on breed and locale). They sport heavily plated scales; lustrous fur at ankle, nape, and tail; and flowing whiskers ready to pick up the slightest tremor in the time-space continuum. They are reptilian, yet mammalian. They fly, yet have no wings. Between paw and jaw they juggle a great pearl, the symbol of the universe. And they smile with the coy self-confidence of a Tibetan fire fox (aka red panda).

The regional similarity of description for Oriental Dragons has lead to wildly varied speculation regarding their genesis and morphology (biological form and function). Early evolutionists were convinced, in the absence of a fossil record to the contrary, that Oriental Dragons—indeed all Dragons—descended from the great cosmic land Dragons of Africa and the Middle East. On the face of things, this made a sort of sense; it was, after all, the path followed by our human ancestors. However, this theory presumes

---

2. Kakuzo, *Awakening of Japan*, 78–79.

Dragons are late arrivals on the global stage, being contemporaries of Homo sapiens at the earliest. Some dracophiles, particularly those with deep ties to the fanciful, have taken this idea even further. In his book *Dragons and Dragon Lore*, Ernest Ingersoll, for example, insists that Dragons did not exist prior to their appearance in recorded history—a notion which, fossils or no fossils, would be laughable if applied to any other species. Following this logic, the track of draconic evolution goes from Egypt to the Middle East to the Far East, then splinters off to Europe and the Western Hemisphere, all within the last 200,000 years. Of course, most of those folks are what we today consider Dragon Creationists, who insist that Dragons are human constructs, a notion about which the Cosmic Creator Dragons would surely have something to say! While it seems a tidy, even noble lineage, it just happens to be wrong.

Ingersoll goes on to insist that Dragons only moved off the Asian mainland in the wake of Chinese exploration and conquest, making Japanese and Korean Dragons offspring at best—poor relations at worst—of the five-toed Chinese Dragon, or *lung*. This too is wrong.

Such errors are all too understandable given the deplorable state of draconic sciences prior to 1900. Until recently, the leading minds in cryptogenetics were trying to force their subjects into an evolutionary model designed for far younger, more mundane species. They were also looking at Dragon evolution from a markedly geocentric perspective, through the eyes of the hordes riding out of Central Asia, assuming they were following in the footsteps of all life before them. While a likely scenario for strictly terrestrial creatures, it is shortsighted when speaking of beings equally at home on land, in the air, and under the sea. Within the last fifty years, speculation about Dragon genesis has become far more liberal and, consequently, more accurate. This is particularly helpful when examining our mysterious Eastern friends, who are believed to stem from the oldest branch on the draconic family tree.

As mentioned in chapter 1, current crypto-evolutionary theory holds that Dragons are the descendants of very, very ancient creatures. Before dinosaurs lived and died, nautical proto-dragons—sea serpents, in the modern vernacular—ruled the oceans, their potent pedigree surviving both the Permian and Cretaceous mass extinctions (250 and 65.5 million years ago, respectively), as well as numerous smaller planetary upheavals. The demands of an aquatic existence would have kept them sleek and swift, able to ride a wave or hunt in an abyss. Their link to water would have been both natural and essential. Just as it is with Oriental Dragons. One look at the form and function of the Japanese Dragon King Ryu-jin, the Indonesian Nogo from the isles of Kalimantan and Sulawesi, not to mention the various mainland Lung, and the similarities to these prehistoric monarchs of the deep become undeniable. One can also see that the Dragons of the Middle East are more akin to Western than Eastern Dragons, indicating a far-from-simple genealogy. Thus, though our human ancestors trekked eastward over desert and frozen steppe, it is very likely the Dragons they met, with muddied paws and salt-tipped manes surfing the Kuroshio Current along the coast of Japan, were coming from the opposite direction.

What must the ancient peoples of Asia have made of these great creatures both familiar and foreign, and unquestionably

Dragon, sporting in the surf and lounging along riverbanks! To the lay person, it's said your average Oriental Dragon looks like a mash-up of snake, lion, stag, and eagle. This is the sort of oversimplification that, while expected from our kind, does little justice to the parties involved. In centuries past, some people have even suggested that Dragons are actually a patch-work creature, a fanciful composite like the centaur or hippogryph. Asian expert and mythologist Dr. M. W. de Visser (1876–1930), in his opus, *The Dragon in China and Japan*, notes that the early philosophical treatise *Hwai Nan Tsze* (second century BCE) flips this idea on its head. Rather than constructing the Dragon from other creatures, it suggests the Dragon is deconstructed, and thus creates all creatures:

> *Hwai Nan Tsze goes as far as to declare . . . : "All creatures, winged, hairy, scaly and mailed, find their origin in the dragon."*[3]

Our understanding of Dragons has improved over the years, and those who've been fortunate enough to meet an Eastern Dragon eye-to-eye dismiss all notions of hybridization or cut-and-paste creature-making as simply Dragon lore in all its glorious imprecision.

To the best of our modern knowledge, the physiological facts of Eastern Dragons are these:

There are three breeds, each virtually identical save for toe count: three, four, or five. Within each breed and even within an enchantment, there are additional variations: flying and flightless, horned and hornless. Further divisions have been imposed upon them by human beings, but these

---

3. Visser, *Dragon in China and Japan*, 64–65.

are matters more of philosophy, even religion, than natural science (see chapter 6). Citing scholar Tung Sze-chang's seventeenth-century discussion of the bodily differences between the sexes, de Visser notes:

> *The male dragon's horn is undulating, concave, steep; it is strong at the top, but becomes very thin below. The female dragon has a straight nose, a round mane, thin scales and a strong tail.*[4]

While visual distinctions between the sexes can be both intriguing and useful, there is little evidence of these differences outside of charming though unsubstantiated tales. One such story tells of a woman and her husband who chastised a famous painter because all his Dragons looked alike. How was an art lover expected to tell male from female? Taking offense as only an artist can, the painter threw down his brushes, demanding to know how they, mere mortals, could possibly know anything about Dragons. "Because we are Dragons," they said, promptly shedding their human form and standing before the dumbstruck man in all their scaly splendor.

Gender differences—or the lack there of—aside, the Chinese flying five-toed is the rarest and grandest of Oriental Dragons, with adults stretching a svelte 30 meters (almost 100 feet) from nose to tail. By comparison, a three-toed Korean Earth Dragon will be barely half that length. Smaller for sure, but still not a Dragon to be taken lightly.

Oriental Dragons reach sexual maturity more slowly than their Occidental or Western counterparts, with ancient

---

4. Ibid., 71.

lore insisting that only Dragons entering their fourth millennium are able to take a mate and reproduce. An absurdity on its face, this fanciful tidbit was used to bolster the belief in Dragons as creatures of otherworldly extremes. Not that they need any help: Dragon truths are easily as impressive as human fictions. In actuality, they are mature at just over a hundred years, with a Queen able to breed every half-century. She will lay a very small clutch of eggs— only two or three—and incubate them devotedly for nearly two years, a good six months longer than other Dragons. Taking natural disasters, poachers, accidents, and the rare spoiled egg into consideration, population explosions are nonexistent. In fact, for all their longevity and parental diligence, a mating pair is lucky to have a half dozen offspring reach maturity and carry on their bloodlines.

At the end of their neatly coiled shell time, the Oriental Dragonlets chip their way into the world, all of 2 meters (6.5 feet) long—mostly tail—and essentially miniature copies of their parents. They are wide-eyed and wide-mouthed, with whiskers twitching and jaws full of pearly teeth eager to sink into their first meal. Tight plating, like the undershell of a turtle, shields their bellies—the better to saunter through forest and marsh—while the layered scales on their back and legs, soft in the egg, quickly harden into armor any samurai would die for. Their ankles, tail, and nape are tufted with thin, yolk-sticky fur, promising future tresses of shaggy distinction.

Adorning broad hatchling brows are two tiny, velvet-covered nubs. For those destined to be horned, these will eventually sprout into impressively gnarled racks. Such head ornaments were once believed to crown only males and be used for display and/or defense; recent studies have found this is not true. As with flight, horns are a simple matter of genetics. Like brown eyes, horns are a dominant trait; like red hair, flight is recessive. Thanks to complicated family relations, within one enchantment—even within one clutch—any combination of traits is possible. Unfortunately, Dragon parts, especially horns, were prized for their presumed medicinal properties—touted as a cure for everything from shingles to madness. In the sixteenth and seventeenth centuries, greedy poachers led to a grievous decline in the Dragon populations of central China. When Dragons were scarce, some people pawned off antlers—especially those of the East Asian Sambar and Père David's deer—as Dragon horns. While the Dragons were no doubt delighted by this turn of events, the practice devastated deer herds, contributing to the Père David's extinction in the wild.

Coloring is also a function of genetics, and newborns reflect the hues of their parents within expected parameters. As Dragons mature, their pigmentation modulates according to environment and diet. Chlorophyll-rich vegetation of the forest makes for lush, mossy Dragons; the minerals in the sea, seaweeds, and fish create Dragons who shimmer like the interior of abalone shells. It was believed that the celestial Dragons fed on meteorites, which bedecked them in the luminescent shades of the heavens—a delightful fancy with little scientific evidence to back it up. In the past, when the land was open and lightly peopled, Dragons were far more mobile and, throughout their lengthy lifetimes, changed color three or four times a year. This mercurial nature was aided in no small part by the regular shedding of their skin. When color-tuned to their environment, an

Eastern Dragon is virtually invisible save to others of their kind and a handful of extremely keen-eyed dracophiles.

In addition to first-class camouflage, these master survivalists are equipped with potent neurotoxins, atomized on their torrid breath and misted over prey and/or enemy with subtle control. Distinguishing judiciously between the need for lethal and non-lethal force, Oriental Dragons will dispatch meals with humane speed. When it comes to foes, they usually go for the knockout rather than the kill, then make a tactical retreat. This keeps animosity between Dragons and their adversaries—i.e., us—at civilized levels and is considered a recognition of the fact that the vast majority of encounters with humans are accidental and/or benign. It also demonstrates the relatively laid-back nature of Oriental Dragons. Indeed, anecdotal evidence insists they are the least quarrelsome of the True species, a trait attributed in large part to the reverence and honor with which they are treated. Though less in the world of men than they once were, these magnificent creatures remain as ancient shaman and sage knew them. They are not only even-tempered but also loyal, playful, slow to anger, and quick to sing. Attentive and great-hearted, they have been known to give us the benefit of the doubt whether or not we deserve it.

That said, for any individual intending harm, the rules are simple: if the law doesn't get you, the enchantments will.

Unnatural History: Cosmological Relevance

From amoeba to Sky Dragon, every creature on Earth knows one thing: water is life.

This is important to remember if you wish to understand the cosmological relevance given Oriental Dragons by the ancient people of the region.

Thirty-five thousand years ago, the last great ice age blanketed the planet. Northern and Central Asia were frozen, arid deserts. How prehistoric peoples survived in these wastelands beggers the imagination, but some did. They lived close to the land, learning deep in their bones its give and take, bounty and want. In time, tired of frostbite and a steady diet of mammoth meat, they left the bitter hardships of the glacial regions behind, following trickles of open water down into southern lowlands and coastal plains. There rivulets turned to rivers, and temperate breezes piped through forests of bamboo.

There they saw Dragons. And everything changed.

The change wasn't due to the mere discovery of the Dragons: Siberian Snow Dragons had lived in the Altai Mountains of Mongolia since the Miocene Epoch (20 million years ago), so their paths would have crossed before. But those were lean and hungry creatures, essentially Western in aspect, struggling to survive in a hostile environment. Their relationship with humans was competitive, even adversarial.

They were nothing like the lowland goliaths humans now encountered. Never had the Stone Agers seen such a magnificently variegated array of Dragons, fit and sassy, the rulers of all they surveyed. Past experience would have taught the foreigners distrust and fear, and they were wise enough to keep a respectful distance. But these creatures radiated a very different aura from their northern cousins. They were bigger, healthier, more joyful than any beings ever known.

The Dragons sang and fish leapt into their paws; they danced upon the clouds and the rains fell warm and sweet and often.

Though the Dragons could have been oblivious—or worse—to this emerging human presence, they chose to welcome the newcomers as cohabitants of their realms. After generations battling long nights and dry, bitter cold, this world of Dragons was a paradise to the wanderers. They gazed upon the majestic creatures commanding the waters and knew they were commanding life itself. That was supernatural by any stretch of the imagination. For mere mortals, to live in the shadow of Dragons was wondrous and, as the essayist Thomas Carlyle wrote, "Wonder is the basis of worship." It was a small leap for these awed people to turn Dragons—or at least representative Dragons—into Givers of Life and Creators of the Universe.

But how does one live among gods who can swallow one whole? Happily, the world was young and resources were plentiful. With shamans acting as go-betweens, the Dragons shared the bounty of land and sea with the human outlanders and taught them civilized lowland ways. In return, weyrs were kept sacred, Dragons worshipped, and stories told.

These earliest Dragon tales were the precursors of primitive cosmologies. They told of the First Dragon, born out of chaos, whose egg cracked open, spilling forth the universe in a Big Bang moment. And of her children, beings thousands of years old, who stretched from Earth to sky and circled the world under the sea, carving rivers with their broad tails and raising mountains with a flick of their talons. And of *their* children, smaller but still divine: Dragons wise and noble, the epitome of power and justice, who spoke every language from tiny musk shrew to humpback whale—all

Dragons are superb linguists—and kept the world balanced, to boot. These were the Dragons humans knew personally and under whose protection they settled. From draconic counsel they learned to fish and farm, to mine the rich land and work its treasures.

Thus began one of the longest lasting and most profound bonds between Dragons and humankind the world has known. True, the connection altered over the centuries, proving almost as changeable as the Dragons themselves. But that was to be expected. People being the far more fruitful species, in the blink of Ryu-jin's eye, small villages became cities, stealing both habitat and sovereignty from the enchantments. Out of myth was fashioned religion and, though Dragons were still revered, gods took on more human aspects (such as Nu Kua and the Jade Emperor). In the process, our friends were relegated to being extras on the cosmic stage: celestial messengers, weather spirits, defenders of wood and stream, and guardians of the new anthropomorphic Creators. (We'll explore this in greater detail in chapter 6.)

For some, especially those wishing to ride into power on the tail-tufts of draconic belief, Dragons thus diminished in stature became more accessible. In time, new stories were told of kingships wrested on claims of potent Dragon blood coursing through human veins. Indeed, the royal families of Japan and China are said to be direct descendants of Dragon Kings. Such assertions, while more fancy than fact, litter the lore from Siberia to Indonesia, an enduring testament to the esteem in which Oriental Dragons were held.

Scholars note that not all Dragons fared so well. Yamato no Orochi of Japan, the wayward son of the Dragon King, was depicted as a right surly brute who terrorized Honshu Island's Idzumo Province, demanding maiden sacrifices for his gastronomic delight. The people of Idzumo were saved when the storm god, Susanoo (himself a bit of a rogue), slew the great Dragon (how this set with Orochi's royal father is anyone's guess!). Contemporary scholars are quick to point out that, while from a rare draconic line, at the time of his demise, Orochi was not only exiled from his father's kingdom but transformed into an eight-headed, eight-tailed pseudo-dragon. This demotion maintains the regal standing of the True Dragons while allowing for an intriguing piece of lore.

Today these powerful beings, though practically out of sight, are not out of mind. Granted, their position in the modern world is more symbolic than divine, but this is a reflection on us, not them. We wear their likenesses in pendants or tattoos, hoping a fraction of their strength and good fortune will rub off on us. We honor their eternal connection to the waters with Dragon-boat regattas and fervent prayers to Shen Lung, Dragon of Rain, in times of drought.

And then there is their place in the heavens. Astrologically speaking, people born in the year of the Dragon are blessed beyond measure. They are natural leaders, fearless, gifted, and charismatic. They can do anything they set their minds to, be it in the arts, sciences, or government; and while they have a short fuse with fools, they are also generous, mystical, and amazingly lucky. (These are the broad strokes. A year's ruling element—wood, fire, earth, metal or water—brings nuance to one's character. See chapter 7.) In short, as much as is humanly possible, these individuals *are* Dragons. Understandably, politicians and generals take it as a sign of greatness to be born under the Dragon's protection. Mao Tse-tung (b. 1893), for example, rode his draconic ambitions to the very pinnacle of power. And monarchs from Yao of the Five Emperors to Genghis Khan have been known to alter their birthdates to avail themselves of the Dragon's power. At the very least, it makes for royal hype that plays well with the masses.

Millennia have come and gone since Stone Age nomads first enjoyed the company of Oriental Dragons. In that time, the continent and everything on it has been shaped and reshaped: glaciers receded and society went from seasonal encampments to sprawling metropolises; wars scarred landscapes and psyches; and hydro-electric projects like the Yali Falls and Three Gorges Dams altered nature in immense ways. To Dragons caught in the middle, such changes were not always welcome. Though appreciation and even reverence for Dragons remained, practically speaking, humanity in its millions and billions discovered they preferred the *idea* of Dragons to the *reality*. The affection bestowed upon Eastern Dragons gives them a leg up on their Western cousins, but being Dragon-friendly is not enough. We humans drove these beings from their ancestral weyrlands and downgraded them from gods to good-luck charms. Worse still, we profaned their very essence by polluting the waterways, overfishing the seas, and infusing the rains with acid. Ernest Ingersoll may have gotten a lot wrong, but he was right about one thing: " ... the cardinal fact [is] that the Oriental dragon stands for 'water.'"[5]

---

5. *Dragons and Dragon Lore*, 36.

Their decreased numbers and the state of their environment are a clarion call for us to do more and do right.

Dragons can't miraculously fix all the world's aquatic ills, yet their place in the interconnectedness of all things wild and natural demands both recognition and reckoning. For the sake of all creatures who rely on the Earth's waters for life and livelihood, we would be wise to remember the Dragons our ancestors knew: the givers, shapers, and protectors of river, rain, and sea. We should remember that where there are Dragons, there the world is healthy and vital; where they are absent, the world is lacking.

Though it comes hard to our species, the natural calamities facing Earth demand we be smart enough to set aside our hubris and entertain the possibility that we don't know everything. And to humbly call on the Dragons for their wisdom and blessings.

If we are as lucky as Dragons, they will listen to our pleas and allow us back in their good graces.

Occidental Dragons

North of the Tropic of Cancer, between Pakistan's snow-capped Hindu Kush and the deep Atlantic, the winds sing with thunder and clouds burn crimson across the horizon. There are Dragons near: solid, winged, flame-hurling guardians of spring and treasure who've played across the Western psyche since early Homo sapiens hunted Germany's Neander Valley and invoked the anima of the wild in paintings on the walls of the caves of Lascaux, France. These are the Western, or Occidental, Dragons you've heard so much about. The splendid Dragons of flight and fire.

Marvels of contradiction, Western Dragons—"Westies" to their friends—have, for millennia, been reviled not revered, persecuted not protected. It is no understatement to say that their Eastern kin lived privileged lives by comparison. And yet today there are more Westies in the wild than any other True species; so many in fact, that some have dared call them "common"—but not to their faces, of course. Their prosperity owes small thanks to us and big thanks to devoted enchantments, strong wings, and boundless draconic curiosity. Sometime after the sixth-century Saxon invasion of Celtic lands, members of the put-upon enchantments headed across the Atlantic and established weyrs in the lightly inhabited New World. The Trans-Atlantic Transmigration, as it's called, was crucial to their self-preservation: not only did it expand their territory, but it provided much-needed sanctuary during what proved to be a near-extinction event in Europe.

But the migration alone does not explain the current Occidental Dragon boom. They've also been helped by a radical shift in attitude towards them over the past 150 years, due in part to a nineteenth-century interest in medievalism and the recent proliferation of New Age and fantasy literature. Though not to be taken as scientific gospel, such whimsical tomes display Dragons with wisdom, elegance, and kindness. Not all of them are positive, of course—Tolkien's Smaug, for example, comes from an older, more malevolent mold (see chapter 8)—but enough good images arose to create a sea change in public opinion, tamp down fears, and make preservation efforts possible. This rich, increasingly accessible pool of friendly individuals is a benefit to research and public relations alike. In stark contrast to the East, Western weyrs are open to both die-hard scientists and casual Dragon lovers. This contact translates into shared knowledge and ever-increasing appreciation.

It also helps that the sight of Dragons on the wing is nothing short of life-altering. Whether you consider them boon or bane, as in the words of Arren, wizard of Ursula Le Guin's Earthsea stories said, "I do not care what comes after; I have seen the dragons on the wind of morning."[6]

Natural History:
Evolution, Morphology, and Temperament

Occidental Dragons are considered the youngest of the True species. In Dragon years, that still makes them exceptionally old. Though impossible to pin to an exact timeline, many cryptoherpetologists believe Westies' ancestors were becoming recognizable approximately 60–50 million years ago. Developing from small, winged proto-species, they emerged from the Cretaceous extinction and started to grow. Not that they had much competition: The dinosaurs were gone and, save for terror birds (large flesh-eating avians, as their name implies), the warm-blooded terrestrial megafauna of the time were mostly herbivorous. (Megacarnivores like cave lions and bears and the large Aussie monitor lizard, *megalania*, came on the scene many millions of years later in the Quaternary Period [2 million years ago].)

By the Middle Eocene (45–35 million years ago), early Western Dragons ruled the land and sky. They enjoyed a diet including grazers like the massive *uintathere* [win'-tah-theer] (ancestor of the rhino) and the plentiful *phenacodus* [fen-ak'-ohduss] (ancestor of the llama); a family might even have brought down a 15-ton *indricothere* [in'dree-koh-theer']

---

6. Le Guin, *Farthest Shore*, 147.

(another rhino ancestor). This megafauna menu helped them grow a good 40 percent larger than their modern descendants. Naturally, as the prey shrank, so did the predators; yet, though size was lost, dominion was not—at least not until the ascent of man and the modern age. The most adaptable of species, Dragons have survived the Sahara Desert's blistering heat and bitter Arctic winds. From the lake country of Saskatchewan to the open steppes of Central Asia, they've staked their claim and called Earth their home.

To the best of our knowledge, the Occidental Dragons we know today are not noticeably different from those of two million years ago. This constancy has given them a place in human racial memory so secure that from child to wizened elder, people around the globe are familiar with a Westie's form and structure. Unfortunately, much of what is assumed about their temperament is rank fiction.

But let's start with the qualities about which there is little doubt.

A full grown Western Dragon stands approximately 3.5 meters (11.5 feet) at the shoulder and is 9 meters (29.5 feet) from nasal plates to coccyx. Tack on another 14 meters (46 feet) of powerful tail and a wingspan of over 27 meters (88 feet) and you have an elegantly proportioned being who turns heads wherever she roams. Males are stockier than females, a fact which enters in when it comes to egg incubation. Like birds, Dragon bones are honeycombed for strength and lightness, an adaptation essential for flight. Their wings are anchored just ahead of the pelvic girdle. This allows the ribbed sails of leathery wing skin to billow with the slightest breeze or thermal.

Smooth or scaly (*smooth* is actually a misnomer: all Dragons are scaly, but some Dragons have smaller scales than others and so appear smooth), heredity dictates the texture and hue of a Dragon's hide. To a lesser degree, heredity also affects their individuating features: horns, neck frills, and tail spades. Though Dragons and meticulous observers can discern familial similarities, such ornamentation is as distinctive as fingerprints and makes for a tapestry of unique individuals.

More prolific than their Oriental cousins, Westie Queens are able to breed in their fourth decade and every twenty-five years thereafter; Sires require an extra ten to twenty years to reach sexual maturity. Careful to keep their gene pool strong, mating within an enchantment is taboo. Thus the importance of multi-enchantment weyrs. When community bloodlines become too diluted, Dragons who wish to mate take to the skies in search of another weyr that will accept them. Though fraught with danger and even death, such ventures are essential to the perpetuation of the species.

Following a long, formal courtship, if all goes well, a pair will make a bond that lasts a lifetime. Though all Dragons bond for life, not all bond to breed. This accommodates individual sexual orientations and serves as a natural check on population growth. Those who do mate will produce a clutch of three to eight eggs (relative to Oriental Dragons, the larger and more frequent broods more than compensate for Westies' somewhat shorter lifespans). Eighteen months later, amid hatching fire and birthing song, the little Dragonlets emerge into the world. Ungainly as any newborn, they totter about as best they can, stretching their fledgling wings in the sun.

Over the next few years the youngsters will be taught the ways of Dragonhood: how to hunt and fish, which plants are savory, which should be avoided. This is a complicated job—especially if a weyr is blessed with several broods in the same season—so everyone is expected to pitch in.

At age two, Westie Dragonlets grow into youthful fire breathing. Their pyronic (fire) sacs—barely noticeable at birth—become fully developed, and their palates become more sophisticated, embracing the foods and minerals necessary to producing flame. The rest is a matter of biology and practice.

When they reach their third year, Dragonlets are old enough to leave their landbound ways and take to the skies. But first they undergo a major physical transformation. Up until now, though their bodies have grown big and strong, their wings have remained disproportionately small. The first step Dragons take towards flight is to shed the soft velvet on their wings—much as a stag removes the plush layer on his antlers—and allow them to emerge in all their leathery glory. This growth spurt, comparable to what we go through in our teens, requires an understandable period of adjustment. Shoulder and flight muscles have to strengthen, and the young ones have to adjust to the resultant shift in their center of gravity. A couple of months of intense training follows, and they are on their way!

It should be noted that for an Occidental Dragon to truly master flight, they must first be fire-proficient—hence their natural progression through the years. Gases not spent in pyrotechnic bravado give them that extra bit of lift that not only eases muscle strain but also helps them travel farther and maneuver with greater dexterity. Despite dramatic images from film and lore to the contrary, this connection between flight and flame inclines Dragons on the wing to use fire as a last resort, especially when young. It does them little good to hurl unrestrained blasts only to be grounded in the process. In time, they learn how to carefully coordinate flame and flight; still, even full-grown Dragons usually opt for the safety of distance over confrontation. But if a fight is unavoidable, they prefer to stay grounded, where with size, flame, and cunning they can employ battle tactics sure to send Alexander the Great running back to boot camp.

Though Dragon physiology won't surprise your average dracophile, the truth about their temperament is another matter. For reasons buried deep in the Western psyche, Dragons have long been ascribed fierce, bloodthirsty natures. They've been portrayed as the most ruthless of monsters: lone beasts killing for no reason, cutting a merciless swath through croft and crop and all things in between. These were the nightmare demons who made maidens scream and gave the bravest of warriors night sweats.

This anti-Dragon propaganda, sifted from centuries of European tales and fears, resembles the truth as much as a gerbil resembles a porcupine. Let's look at the facts.

Not as laid-back as Oriental Dragons, our intelligent winged friends are, at the best of times, gregarious, even rowdy. They enjoy the company of their kind and others and, while individuals have been known to strike out on their own, they are the exception, not the rule, usually driven to such a lifestyle by the human destruction of weyr and clan. Westies are devoted family Dragons who will protect kith and kin with their lives—including the humans under their wings. That said, they are not warm and fuzzy (okay, they are warm); this is a commercial notion put forth by Saturday-morning TV and is nothing short of insulting.

They are highly territorial, especially when there are hatchlings about and, like other Dragons (and most mundane creatures), will not shy from using every means at their disposal to keep unwanted intruders at bay. Adages about poking sleeping Dragons are some of the more accurate bits of lore handed down through the ages. Still, unless otherwise distressed, they take a good deal of prodding. In light of how we have treated them, their lack of unprovoked aggression is nothing short of amazing.

When dealing with Western Dragons, we would do well to remember that despite their power and fierce outward aspect, they are extraordinary sentient beings, in ways not dissimilar to ourselves. That they have been feared rather than exalted in the manner of the Eastern Lung and Ryu-jin speaks to limitations of Western perception and culture. We chose to see monsters, fearsome, wild, and bloody. Let reason temper our fancy and we could see them as they truly are—the way more and more people are finally seeing them: as marvelously passionate pieces of the natural mosaic.

If we treat them with due caution, deference, and open eyes, we'll find a little awe can banish a world of fear.

Unnatural History: Cosmological Relevance

Monsters, monsters everywhere!

This was the cry of Harald Bluetooth's sorcerer when he returned from scouting the fjords of Iceland for his liege. According to the *Heimskringla* sagas, it was the tenth century, and Bluetooth was keen on invading the isle, wresting it from the few Norse inhabitants who called it home. But Bluetooth was also cautious: before committing men and resources, he sent his magus on a reconnaissance mission to find the island's vulnerable spots. In whale-guise, the sorcerer explored the rugged coastline; yet every time he approached land, he saw hills and rivers rife with *landvættir*—nature wights—fiercely protecting the island. The first and most terrifying of the wights was the huge Dragon Dreki.[7] The people worshipped him and he kept them safe, which seemed a fair exchange. Dreki rumbled down to the shore, a swarm of snakes, lizards, and toads in his wake. He huffed and puffed great billows of noxious vapor at the wizard, driving him off into the frigid Atlantic. The invasion was called off; even a Christian king like Harald Bluetooth knew not to cross otherworldly draconic forces.

Though late to the European record, Dreki was emblematic of the cosmic Dragons of the West. They were fierce, dark creatures with wings big enough to blot out the sun and jaws wide enough to swallow worlds whole. They drank the oceans dry and bound the Earth in their coils. Vitra of India and Ophion of ancient Greece, Jörmungandr and Niðhögger from Nordic realms: they were creators and destroyers, servants and foes of both gods and men. Good and bad, taken as cosmological phenomena, they were beings more of power than of magic. (The magic came later when Druids and alchemists dealt with mortal enchantments. See chapters 6

---

7. Though *landvættir* come in all shapes and sizes, in Iceland there are four major guardians of the isle's spirit corners, Dreki (NE), Gammur the Gryphon (NW), Griðungur the Bull (SW), and Bergrisi the Giant (SE). Not unlike the four cosmic beasts of which Ezekiel dreamt, with the coming of Christianity, the quartet was readily adapted. Of course, turning a Dragon into an eagle is a radical comedown. Many Icelanders prefer the originals, even today.

and 7.) Most lacked the sophistication of their Eastern cousins, displaying unrefined energy and raw fury rather than meditative wisdom. And yet, especially up north, Occidental Dragons suited the rough-and-tumble Europeans to a T, their fearless, ferocious natures embraced by warriors and chieftains throughout their range.

To properly understand Western Dragons' role in the cosmic scheme of things, it is important to know that their divinity was defined by a take on creation far less nature-based than that of the East. Dragons were good enough to carve out rivers and raise mountains, even form the Earth out of their flesh, but when it came time to shape humanity, the Indo-European peoples ultimately wanted gods they could relate to—i.e., gods who looked like them. This diminished the divine fear factor considerably. Not that it was done away with entirely; there is something to be said for the need to quake before our gods. If they don't inspire the shivers how can we be expected to take them seriously? Yet Dragons were a bit over the top for Western sensibilities. One look at them and their wildness pours through, putting the ill-informed and faint-hearted in full-on panic mode. In the end, they proved just too stressful for everyday wear. But we run ahead of ourselves.

At an earlier age, Dragons were all that stood between the void and the world. This was the time of the great Chaos Dragons: Tiamat and her attendant Zu, Rahab and the ravenous Apophis. From Egypt to the Fertile Crescent, they formed something out of nothing, setting the stage for the anthropomorphic deities to come.

According to the Sumerian scripture, *Enuma Elish* (c. 1100 BCE), Tiamat and Zu were, respectively, the salt and freshwater Dragons of the primordial universe.[8] Tiamat was the personification of Creative excess, her children such a handful that Zu plotted to do away with them for the survival of the Universe. He failed at this, being slain instead by his son Ea, whose son, Marduk the sky god, in turn rose up and slew his grandmother, forming the world—land and ocean—out of her remains. An unruly lot, that first family. And yet, according to some, the spilt blood of Zu mixed with the land and humans were formed out of that potent slurry. Thus people, even in such a dracophobic realm, are the children of Dragons.

Another cosmic water Dragon, Rahab, made his way into the Psalms of the Old Testament:

> *Thou [God] rulest the raging of the sea: when the waves thereof arise, thou stillest them.*
> *Thou hast broken Rahab in pieces, as one that is slain: thou hast scattered thine enemies with thy strong arm.*[9]

Of a slightly different stripe, Apophis was a voracious moon Dragon out of ancient Egypt. He emerged from the cosmic void with a terrifying roar and dined on unlucky souls journeying between this life and the next. Even the sun god Ra was vulnerable to this great Dragon and was occasionally caught in his mighty jaws. Fortunately for the world, Ra left a bad taste in the creature's mouth and was soon vomited back into the sky. Situations that could have

---

8. Though viewed in a less benevolent light than in the East, water is again essential to Creation. Of course, that part of the world was not as arid as it is today and water could have been seen as a disruptive force. See King, "The Seven Tablets of Creation, Enuma Elish."

9. Psalms 89:9–10.

resulted in permanent darkness wound up being simple yet awe-inspiring eclipses.

No one knows exactly when the influence of these great Cosmic Dragons began to wane. Recent archaeological finds in Göbekli Tepe near Urfa, Turkey, show considerable demotion by 9000 BCE, with draconic figures serving as decorative totems rather than full-fledged deities of the temple.[10] This represents a major shift in human cultural and social structure, with people on the verge of leaving the fearful uncertainty of hunter-gatherer lives and entering an age of domesticated animals, planted fields, and established towns. We were pulling ourselves out of the natural order, wrapping ourselves in the evolving cloak of civilization. Dragons who embodied the power of wildness had little place in such a human-centered environment.

But what to do with them?

It fell to new humanized deities to challenge the old draconic ones. Marduk slew Tiamat, Eurynome banished Ophion, Yahweh conquered Rahab. By the age of King Gilgamesh (c. 2500 BCE), the old Cosmic Dragons were fading; by the time of the Olympians (600 BCE), they were no more. The new gods hugged their Chaos long and hard until it melted away in their hands. Those Dragons who remained within the mythic realm had two options: be divine servants, such as Ladon guarding Hera's golden apples and the Dragon in Eden coiled round the Tree of Life; or be monsters, such as Gandareva of Sumer, filling the populace with fear and loathing until dispatched (as they always were) by a prince-

---

10. Curry, "Göbekli Tepe: The World's First Temple?"

ling out to prove he had divine blood in his veins. Not much of a choice for the descendants of beings who once stretched across the heavens and lit the stars with Dragonfire.

It should also be noted that many Dragons who defended sacred springs and groves were seen as just lackeys of the gods, receiving divine protection for their labors. Of course, if they chose to follow their fiercely independent natures, well, this was considered the height of cosmic insubordination—you don't want to anger the gods!—and merited stripping Dragons of their remaining divinity. Oh, Dragons were still large and dangerous, but they were no longer protected by the taboo against killing deities. It did not matter that these creatures had given men fire or taught priests the secrets of creation. (In a mythic parallel, the Greek Prometheus, another fire-giver, was also bound by the new gods, leading some in draconic circles to swear the Titan had more Dragon blood in him than a thousand puny princelings.) Would-be heroes could now slay them with impunity. So it was that a draconic gloom fell over the Neolithic Mediterranean (c. 8000 BCE), foretelling even darker times to come (see chapter 6).

By the third millennium BCE, Central and Northern Europe were ripe for this anti-Dragon shift, and it spread virtually unchecked from the Balkans to the Arctic Circle. A trending theory among cryptoherpetologists suggests that an influx of people from the Kurgan cultures of the Asian Steppes also contributed to less than sympathetic views of Dragons. Like the ancient Siberians, the Kurgans' experience would have put them in direct conflict with enchantments for food and shelter, tainting their appreciation considerably. The late Neolithic Europeans would have recognized such encounters as grim mirrors of their own troubles. Add to that their demotion in the south, and it was little wonder the mystical Dragons of the region were not welcomed as wild, underappreciated creative forces. Quite the contrary. They were cast as ill-tempered, apocalyptic "beasts" impatiently awaiting the end of the universe. Gods and humans alike viewed them with a toxic mixture of contempt and fear and treated them as outcasts, unfit to live in the same world. Unpleasant temperaments were the result of this abuse. And was it any wonder? Pull a tabby's tail and she will scratch you; enslave a Dragon for eternity and he will eat you—if given the chance, that is.

The giant figures of Nordic lore, Jörmungandr and Niðhögger, are the best known of these dark cosmological Dragons, their malignant personae reflective of the unforgiving world around them. Niðhögger is the older of the two, so old that his pedigree is lost in an age before the gods. He dwells in the Underworld, his body wrapped around the roots of Yggdrasil, the great tree that supports the nine worlds of the Universe. Day after day, he gnaws on the tree's roots, an active participant in the end of the world. As the Norse Eddas (thirteenth-century collections of myth and lore) tell it, Niðhögger breaks free from his tangled cage come Ragnarök, the Twilight of the Gods. He flies over blood-soaked fields, gorging himself on those slain in the last battle. His moniker, Corpse Render, is well earned in the end.

Jörmungandr is a younger, more aggressive Dragon. He was born from the union of the wicked god Loki and his sometime paramour, Angrboða, a lineage that gave him supernatural strength and an ugly disposition. His mood wasn't helped by the fact that his very presence so horrified the gods that they tossed him out of the divine realm of Asgard into the ocean. Now, Dragons are proud and do not take slights lightly; a great grudge was born from this action. In the ocean Jörmungandr grew, as Dragons do, until he circled the whole of Miðgard, the world of men. Clenching his tail tight in his teeth, he holds the world together until the end of days, when all the evils on Earth rise up against men and gods—Jörmungandr included. With apocalyptic bravado, he stormed out of the sea, his wrathful appetite loosed upon all. In an act of mutual sacrifice, the thunder god Thor killed the Dragon, who, in turn, killed Thor. The world ended with a bang only to be born again. A little better, this time.

When Christianity pushed the old Norse gods into the harmless world of faërie tales, they took many a Dragon with them. Niðhögger, however, remained a fierce Underworld figure, reborn (like the world around him) into a dispenser of justice at Satan's side. All fang and claw, he would punish the wicked, using divine retribution that would make the Furies of Greece pale by comparison.

So it was that, with a synchronicity that no doubt tickled them, Cosmic Westies found themselves reluctant participants at both the beginning and end of creation. Bruised and abused for centuries, they put up with indignities no Eastern Dragon ever would. Only after shedding their divine mantle were they able to begin to lose their terrifying reputations. Bit by bit, they reentered the world of men, cautiously approaching people wise enough to appreciate the gifts they had to offer. These wonderful creatures were even generous enough to give us a chance to atone for our litany of past wrongs.

It was a long haul but, at last, modern Western Dragons have gotten to a place where they can be who they are, not who some narrow-minded humans think they should be. They can relish their fearfulness with glee and surprise us with their beauty, loyalty, and affection. We, on the other hand, still have a lot of groveling to do.

But that is another chapter of Dragon history.

four

Feathered Dragons

Nothing keeps creatures quite so safe as an impenetrable environment. And, until recently, nothing was quite so impenetrable as the rain forests of the New World. It is no small wonder that newcomers believed the lustrous Feathered, or Southern, Dragons of the region to be fictions concocted by the indigenous peoples to frighten off invaders. They were Europeans, after all, from a continent increasingly skeptical about Dragons. Used to meadows and deciduous woods, they kept their eyes to the ground, watching for bushmasters, jaguars, and other dangers. Even if they *had* peered into the canopy, chances are they would have seen nothing untoward—certainly not masked Dragons perched atop kapok trees.

While such obscurity may have kept the Dragons out of conquistador sights, it did little to further our understanding of the species. The lack of firsthand scientific observation is staggering. Not that the military men and priests charged with mapping and conquesting knew much about science; surviving accounts by explorers of the time are full of creatures that would try the most whimsically minded suspension of disbelief: Ferdinand Magellan (1480–1521) reported 12-foot-tall giants in Patagonia; Sir Walter Raleigh (1552–1618) boasted of encounters with the Ewaipanoma, headless natives with eyes popping out of their shoulders and mouths in their bellies; and of course Francisco de Orellana (1511–46), the first European to travel the length of the Amazon, recounted run-ins with fierce long-haired— presumably female—warriors who wound up giving the great river its name.

But no Dragons.

In the seventeenth and eighteenth centuries, colonization trumped study. Great trees were felled; indigenous peoples, fauna, and flora were enslaved, relocated, and killed. Watching from above, the Feathered Dragons were secure in the fact that the rain forests were vast, their destruction beyond the means of such scrawny bipeds. They could not foresee the Industrial Age, with its chainsaws and earthmovers ripping through their home. Plumes blushing in the copper sun, Feathered Dragons chose to drift farther into the shrinking forests and deeper into legend.

By the mid-nineteenth century, science saw the uncharted acres of the New World as a laboratory waiting to be explored. In the 1830s, on his way to the Galapagos Islands, naturalist Charles Darwin (1809–82) climbed the mountains of Tierra del Fuego and studied mud-dauber wasps in Brazil and fossils in Argentina; in 1839, amateur archaeologist and diplomat John Lloyd Stephens and artist Frederick Catherwood poked around the Central American ruins of Copan and Palenque, reintroducing the world to the Maya; and conservationist Cândido Rondon embraced the rain forests in earnest, traveling Brazil's River of Doubt with Teddy Roosevelt in 1914. They saw plenty of wildlife but no Dragons (save a few carved in Mayan stone). Despite all these eyes examining their realms, casual Feathered Dragon sightings remained few and far between.

Today, though scientific interest in their environment is peaking, such studies tend to focus on how tropical treasures can benefit mankind. Far less generous commercial assaults on the world's rain forests are catastrophic for all indigenous life forms, including the Feathered Dragons. Preservation efforts cannot stay ahead of deforestation, and verifiable Dragon sightings are becoming as rare as goblins in Central Park. A handful of pessimistic scientists have even suggested they've been driven to extinction. Crypto-herpetologists vehemently deny this heart-rending prospect, despite the fact no comprehensive enchantment count has been taken in decades. Diminished though they are, one hopes the rain forests are still too large and unexplored to make such dire statements. With their ability to blend into the world around them, Feathered Dragons personify the ruling creed of crypto studies: "Just because you can't see something doesn't mean it isn't there."

Natural History:
Evolution, Morphology, and Temperament

Emerging onto the world stage after the Triassic–Jurassic Extinction (200 million years ago), Feathered Dragons are the middle child of the Big Three, and, like many middle children, they can be easily overlooked. Though not as demanding as Eastern and Western Dragons, they nonetheless have much to offer.

In keeping with the Oriental misconception of dinosaur bones belonging to Dragons, scientists long believed Feathered Dragons were an offshoot of feathered dinosaurs, both avian and terrestrial. We know now that they actually evolved from the small proto-dragons who roamed across the southern supercontinent, Gondwana, roughly 180 million years ago. These scrappy creatures used their agility and intelligence to survive among giants. In time, they took to the trees where, with more safety and less competition, they thrived. They grew light, strong bones; sinuous necks; prehensile tails that gripped the branches like a fifth paw; and wings layered with brilliant feathers. Having the advantage of flight, they were able to establish themselves from one end of the supercontinent to the other, nurtured by the huge river/forest system that cut through its heartland. (At the time, the Amazon and the Congo rivers were one, creating a lush world ripe for Dragons and multitudes of fauna, great and small.)

A hundred and thirty million years ago, Gondwana split into Africa and South America, and the realm of the Feathered Dragon became transoceanic; rain forests are rain forests regardless of which side of the Atlantic they occupy. Over millennia, the enchantments of the New World grew strong, with weyrs ranging from the slopes of Mexico's Popocatépetl to the Paraná River delta in what is now Argentina. Scattered lore aside, in the Old World the history of these plumed beauties is obscure at best. For reasons about which we can only speculate, nary a feathered soul has been documented in Africa since before 1856, when Sir Richard Burton and John Hanning Speke searched for the Nile's source and gazed upon the Mountains of the Moon. Contentious and controversial as their expedition was, the reports both men made to the Royal Geographical Society contained no mention of Dragons, feathered or otherwise. Though Old World extinction is the logical conclusion, cryptoherpetologists still live in hope.

What we know of Feathered Dragon morphology and temperament we owe to a handful of dedicated cryptozoologists and logical extrapolation from lore and oral histories. As expected, shimmering plumage is the Feathered Dragon's most conspicuous distinction to the lay observer, yet it is not the only physical trait setting them apart from their Eastern and Western kindred. The demands and limitations of their habitat have made them far and away the smallest of the True Dragons, measuring little more than 9 meters (29.5 feet) long when full grown, with a wingspan between 6 and 7 meters (19 and 23 feet). They are also the lightest of the three species, weighing in at less than 150 kilos (330 pounds). Lithe and agile, they dance through dense stands of rubber trees and mahogany, with feet tucked close lest they clip the branches. Flying serpents silhouetted against the horizon— just imagine! Dragon feathers that fall to the forest floor are usually mistaken for harpy eagle or hornbill plumes. Though a trained cryptoherpetologist can tell the difference, this happy coincidence keeps hunters and the annoyingly draco-curious at bay. Conversely, kings and warriors wishing to lay claim to draconic authority were not above passing off mundane feathers in their possession for those of more extraordinary origins.

Of the big three, arboreal status is the Feathered Dragons' alone. It gives them an aloof quality that complements their inherent shyness. The canopy is a buffer zone in which they can hide, hunt, and carouse at their leisure. In the play of light and shadow, they all but disappear, exemplifying Leonardo da Vinci's observation:

The varieties in the colours of the shadows are as numerous as the varieties in the colour of the objects that are in the shadows.[11]

For a man who'd never crossed the Atlantic, Leonardo's writings on color and light display an uncanny appreciation of Feathered Dragons in all their rainbow glory.

Retiring though they may be, Feathered Dragons are still all Dragon and, as such, are the undisputed rulers of their realm, safe from all but the most lawless of humans out to make a name for themselves as dragon slayers. Back when Chichén Itzá was no more than a mound of unstacked stone in a Yucatan clearing, they dove beneath crystal cenotes and fished the open shallows off Cozumel.

Forest living means fire is not a viable defense, so Feathered Dragons rely on venom instead. When less lethal measures suffice, their whippish tails not only anchor them to

---

11. Da Vinci, *Notebooks*.

moss-slick limbs but also lash their foes with crippling force. And of course, no one can outmaneuver a Dragon on the wing. Aside from abundant rains, the climate is mild enough that weyrs are little more than scrapes and rocky overhangs for all but nesting pairs. An expectant couple will take up residence in labyrinthine burrows carved into sandstone cliff sides and remote plateaus, like the Gran Sabana of eastern Venezuela. There, out of the pounding downpours and blistering sun, the Queen hatches her brood.

Clutch size and length of incubation are just a couple of Feathered Dragon unknowns, their communal nesting sites complicating matters to the point where scientists are left with (barely) educated conjectures in place of hard facts. At best guess, a Queen lays one to three eggs that are nurtured for almost a year. The hatchlings emerge covered with a fine down and are armed with fully functional venom glands. The down is soon replaced by proper feathers except on legs and bellies, which are protected by tight-knit scales. Feathered Dragons take to the air in months, not years, a necessity of survival given their size and penetrable outer covering. It is quite possible flocks presumed to be macaws or quetzals are actually fledgling Dragonlets skimming the river beds and frolicking through the forest.

Feathered Dragon diets are more heavily vegetarian than any other species. How could they not be, surrounded by a smörgåsbord of fruits, nuts, flowers, and greens? Such bounty is supplemented with animal proteins from fish, monkeys, tapirs, even rhea eggs (not as big as their ostrich kin, but a close second). In short, they eat whatever strikes their fancy. They are also suspected of scavenging now and then, though not enough to step on the toes of the king vulture and jabiru stork, supreme scroungers of the region. This helps keep the forest clean, and, by scattering pollen and dispersing seeds, they are instrumental in maintaining the vitality of the ecosystem.

We just have to get out of the way and let Dragons do what they do best.

Unnatural History: Cosmological Relevance

Talk to any child psychologist and they will tell you kids in the middle always try harder. Feathered Dragons live up to this maxim in spades. While their more famous cousins were servants to human gods, the Feathered Serpents and their subsequent incarnations were prime movers and shakers of Mesoamerican Creation.

In the beginning, for example, there was Campacti, a chaos Dragon in the mold of Tiamat (see pages 50–51, chapter 3), whose sacrifice was demanded for the greater good. Out of his massive corpse the world was made—though the "hero" who took him out remains conspicuously anonymous. Unlike the Mesopotamians, who raised cults and nations around their dragon slayers, ancient cultures on the other side of the globe put the sacred Feathered Serpents ahead of emergent humans. Their Dragons were complete beings: all plumes and scales, divine and mundane, air and earth. They were lords of the universe, top to bottom.

From the Olmec to the Aztec, all ancient Mesoamericans honored the Feathered Dragons, but no one worshipped them like the Maya. According to the Mayan book of creation, the *Popol Vuh*, once the basics of land and sea were in place, it fell to the great Sovereign Plumed

Serpent—Q'uq'matz—and the divine triad, Heart of Sky, to refine and populate the world.[12] With the fecundity of their breath, they were makers, modelers, bearers, and begetters.[13] They designed the first universe and the first creatures in all their curious diversity. But something was wrong. The people were wooden manikins, without blood or lymph or mindfulness. They could not honor their creators or keep their days because they could not remember them. The gods may not have been looking for perfection, but this early experiment in humanity fell far short of their divine expectations. Even Geppetto had fared better with his wooden boy! Of course, one of the perks of godhood is the ability to wipe the slate clean and try again. And again.

Obviously, Mayan comprehension of evolution was millennia ahead of its time. They looked upon the monkeys of the forest and saw in their eyes the reflection of the cosmic continuum and the first, imperfect humans. For these were the cycles of creation, the ongoing evolution of the world and all the beings in it, including humans. Including Dragons.

Eventually, like all good parents, the gods had to stop tinkering, step back, and let their children go, flaws and all.

---

12. *Popol Vuh*, 64.

13. Giving a nod to Dragon unity and the cosmic creatures on the other side of the Atlantic, in Mayan ballcourt markers, Q'uq'matz is often represented carrying the sun god Tohil across the heavens in his mouth. In an instance of parallel lines intersecting, the cosmology of western Africa's Fon people celebrates the Creator, Mawu, and her draconic companion, Aido Hwedo. From the snug confines of Aido Hwedo's mouth, Mawu inspected her newly made world, top to bottom, heaven to earth. Q'uq'matz and his Fon counterpart went on to play distinctive roles in their respective Creations, but their similarities—reminders of just how small the world of Dragons can be—continue to give dracophiles pause.

To the creators of the Mayan universe, their newly emptied nest meant they could shift gears—even shift shapes—and pursue other interests. Some of the first makers faded into the cultural background, but not the Sovereign Plumed Serpent. Incarnation after incarnation, she just didn't know how to quit us. Bedecked in blues and greens of sky and land, in guises specific to each city and kingdom, she monitored the two-legs' progress, aiding them when and if the spirit moved her. As the wise Dragon Itzamna [eht zam' na], she gave humans writing and books. As the benevolent Dragon Lakin Chan, she shared herb lore, medicine, and the food of the gods: cacao and the exquisite *xocolatl* [show kow' latl], which Europeans changed into chocolate. In a coincidence not lost on cryptoherpetologists—or Lakin Chan, for that matter—cacao pods look remarkably like immature Dragon eggs. Many steeped in the lore of cacao cuisine carry this draconic theme even further, insisting a proper mole sauce is the consistency and near-black color of Dragon's blood. Some chefs go so far as to say the flavors should dance across the tongue with the burning sweetness of Dragon tears.

Arguably, the most powerful latter-day Feathered Dragon is the Vision Serpent. Conjured during blood rituals, the fiercely wide-mouthed creature served as a direct conduit between divine and mundane realms. In moments of ceremonial ecstasy, the king merges with the Vision Serpent while ancestors and deities—advisors from the hidden worlds—literally speak to the people from the Dragon's mouth. In the thunderous resonance reserved for Dragon and God, this was the voice of unquestionable authority, of wisdom unfettered by time or species. Much as the oracle Pythia of Greece adapted the prophetic words of the Dragon at Delphi to suit a supplicant's needs, so did the Mayan royals interpret the Vision Serpent according to the needs of their people. At times the Dragon served as a counselor of war, all fury and bluster and prophet of great sacrifice. Other times he was mercy and justice personified, full of temperate words dripping with diplomacy. It was an exalted monarch who could listen with care and act accordingly. In stone and ink, this complex communion among Dragon, gods, and men was celebrated with stylized elegance. Bearded and plumed, the Vision Serpent was depicted perched in the World Tree, binding the universe together with coils tightly wrapped from root to topmost limb, just as the counsel threading forth from his mouth binds the people in custom and belief.

While the civilizations in the dense tropics of the Yucatan, Chiapas, and what is now Belize and Guatemala were particularly touched by Feathered Dragon generosity, such blessings were also known north and inland, from the craggy slopes of the Sierra Madre to the dry uplands of the Altiplano of Zacatecas [zah-kah-tay'-kess] in central Mexico.[14] This was the home of Quetzalcoatl [ket-sal'-koh-ah-tul], Feathered Serpent of the Teotihuacán [tay-oh-tee'-wah-kan'] and Aztec people. Be careful not to confuse him with the *Quetzalcoatlus*, a large pterosaur soaring over southern North America some 68 million years ago. Named in honor of the great Feathered Serpent—and even referred to as the Dragon of the Clouds—

---

14. Though Dragons are a part of the Moche and Inca cultures of South America, they did not carry the divine weight of their Mesoamerican kin. For example, modern Dragons are known to sport up and down the Nazca Lines, yet they are never credited with their creation. That is a task humans more incredulously ascribe to extraterrestrials.

his blood ran pure dinosaur with not a smidgeon of Dragon. In contrast to this impressive reptile, the brilliant plumed Dragon was god, messiah, and force of nature. He gave life, laughter, health, and all the arts and sciences a civilization could require, from planting maize to playing music. It is said he mixed his own blood with powdered bone, kneading it into cosmic dough from which he fashioned human beings. His fiery breath baked them just right, turning their skin a golden hue. Then there was hero mode, in which he was often a trickster, shifting shape as the task demanded and triumphing by way of cunning more often than brawn—not that his brawn wasn't formidable when he chose to use it. Quetzalcoatl was a Dragon, after all.

The role of messiah—complete with resurrection—suited Quetzalcoatl less well. In the manner of most ancient tales, the facts have gotten muddied over time, but the basics are these:

After much trial and error, the world was made and populated by man and beast. Integral to these events were Quetzalcoatl and his counterpart, Tezcatlipoca [tez-kat-lee-poh'-kah]. Light and dark, they were; day and night, life and death. It was as it should be, the two working together to bring balance to their creation. Not that there weren't bumps along the way and even major disagreements. The world was destroyed many times over by one or the other in their quest for perfection; but in the end, they came together to reshape a battered universe and initiate the Fifth Sun, the age of modern man.

Unfortunately, as with people, so with gods: with their creative duties behind them, the two became restless and quarrelsome. Tezcatlipoca was particularly peevish, taking cruel exception to the feeble, bloodless offerings made to the feathered one. Where was the sacrifice in the jade and flowers gifted to Quetzalcoatl? And if a fellow god was satisfied with so little, why would people willingly give more to him? His resentment rising to a god-slaying pitch, Tezcatlipoca believed the only way to claim savage tribute was by erasing his gentle rival entirely. One thing led to another, and he tricked his former-cohort-turned-nemesis into the depths of despair. Knowing no other way to stop the pain, the great Feathered Dragon threw himself on a funeral pyre. A flock of birds—quetzals, most likely—flew forth from the flames, carrying his heart into heaven. There, as Venus, the Morning and Evening Star, he watched over a world turned blood-soaked in his adversary's name, a world that ripped the heart from the chests of young priests in tribute to the dark god.

As is so often the case, absence only magnified the Feathered Serpent's cultural and spiritual influence (which must have driven Tezcatlipoca around any number of bends!). At the time of the Aztecs' greatest need, when even divinely inspired warriors came up short, Quetzalcoatl would return, or so the stars and divinations said. The priests envisioned him resurrected à la King Arthur or Jesus, saving the people and ushering the world into the next great age. Unfortunately, prophesy is not an exact science, especially when the element of human interpretation plays such a central role. In the end, a series of crossed signals and shoddy soothsaying led Montezuma to mistake Hernán Cortés for the Plumed Savior in 1519. This seems absurd on so many levels, yet it's important to remember that, in keeping with Cosmic Dragon lore, shapeshifting is a known perk of the job.

If Quetzalcoatl chose to return as a pale human mounted on a horse and covered in burnished silver skin, who were mortals to question him? While this second coming did not unfold as divined, the seers were right about one thing: the Aztec world was driven into a strange, new, post-apocalyptic age that left little room for Dragons or the people who honored them.

Recent linguistic and archaeological studies have greatly expanded our knowledge of Mesoamerican cultures. For cryptomythologists, this new knowledge led to a dispute about which came first: Aztec Quetzalcoatl or Maya Sovereign Plumed Serpent. As fascinating as this might be in a moot, academic sort of way, in the draconic arc of time, it really doesn't matter. The Teotihuacan was the oldest civilization, the Aztec the youngest, and both interacted with the Maya. Similarities in regional iconography and architecture attest to a free-flowing exchange of ideas, skills, and beliefs. More to the point, Olmec or Aztec, king or farmer or child, when the people looked up, they saw Dragons. Glistening in the sun, these feathered wonders whorled between land and cloud; their songs vibrated through forested hills, more magnificent than anything the humans had ever heard. They were incomparable power, raw and unrestrained, next to which all other gods looked pale and inadequate.

The centuries have not been kind to the indigenous flora and fauna of the New World, Dragons and humans included. In the back of the rain forest beyond, species are vanishing before they're even discovered. Yet the pervasiveness of Cosmic Feathered Dragons leads to the inevitable conclusion that, though rare today, they once ruled the Americas from the headwaters of Mexico's Rio Balsas to the roiling cataracts of Rio Iguaçu in Argentina. That's enough space for even Dragons to get lost in.

So, brew yourself a cup of chocolate, dark, frothy, and liberally infused with chili and cinnamon—*xocolatl* Lakin Chan would have sipped with pleasure. Follow the steamy, fragrant plumes rising into the air. There you'll find the hope of Feathered Dragons waiting to be discovered anew.

five

Pseudo-Dragons

Varied though breeds of True Dragons are, they all con-
form to certain physical and cultural standards and to
certain codes of behavior. The same cannot be said of the
plethora of lesser or pseudo-dragons, who are quite literally all over the map with respect to habitat, physique, and
temperament.

Small-*d* pseudo-dragons are a collection of strange,
vaguely reptilian crypto species that, across millennia of
history and lore, have found themselves lumped into the
broad draconic fold. Some were hybrid variations on the
great serpents and lizards that rumbled across the land,
sporting attributes both ominous and mystical. Others
were the stuff of human fears exaggerated into myths that

adorned banners and crests, the tales of their oft-villainous exploits keeping more than a few children up at night.

While many species have vanished in the wake of habitat devastation and celebrity-hungry dragon slayers, the echoes of their existence survive in legend and whispers of mutated DNA. Both far-ranging and extremely localized, species have been known to vary significantly from area to area. It has been said their adaptability rivals that of Charles Darwin's finches, though those seed eaters are much safer to study. When it comes to physical diversity, pseudo-dragons run the gamut with flair: winged and wingless, mammoth and minute, elegant and gangly. They fill the niches of the crypto studies, providing alluring species for virtually every taste. From legless wyrms to the rare eight-legged *piernas cuélebre* of the Pyrenees, they claim variety as their birthright, and are a celebration of the diversity of the crypto world. (By the by, most cryptoherpetologists acknowledge that the *piernas cuélebre* have been extinct since the end of the Spanish Civil War, the last sighting reported by a band of *maquis* partisans crossing the Pyrenees in 1940.)

Though pseudo-dragons refuse to play by any established rules, there are a few guidelines we should follow when in their presence. First and foremost, remember: large or small, benign or hostile, all pseudo-dragons are potentially dangerous. All of them have serious teeth and talons that can deliver crippling—even deadly—injuries. Additionally, some have toxins, some caustic blood, some stony stares. Like snakes, the poisonous species are both front- and rear-fanged. Also like snakes, their venom is designed primarily for hunting: heavy-duty hemo-, cyto-, and neurotoxins which can drop a meal many times their size in a heartbeat. The front-fanged types tend to be the most aggressive of the lot. They have a heightened sense of territory, and are easily frightened and quick to react. Though they can adjust their poison discharge to suit their prey, they are not discreet when threatened. Almost never giving a dry bite, they choose instead to inject copious quantities of venom into their foe. Just to be sure.

With few exceptions, pseudo-dragons are indiscriminate carnivores. If they eat veggies at all, it is more as an afterthought than a conscious dietary decision. This makes even the least of the lot as essential as owl, python, and leaf-nosed bat when it comes to rodent and insect control. (If only we would treasure them in this role, instead of clinging to our ancient fears!) Unfortunately, many have cast the larger ones—hydras, wyverns, various drakes, and water dragons, to name a few—as potential man-eaters. Chances are that such reports are more myth than truth, but don't count on it. Better safe than sorry.

Finally, always be mindful that the lesser species are far less complex and intelligent than True Dragons, more on the level of a bush baby than a human being. This is true even of the most mystical pseudo-dragons and is offered without judgment. It's just the way things are. Adhering more closely to the ways of mundane lizards and serpents, for example, pseudo-dragons tend to be loners, coming together to mate and perhaps nest, then going their separate ways. In keeping with this social template, most pseudo-dragon youngsters are self-sufficient within a week of hatching—some right out of the egg—eager to scamper off and make their mark on the world. They also function on a more instinctive, less rational level than True Dragons; their fight or flight urges are fine-tuned and lightning fast.

An Overview of Specific Species

Though Dragon snobs consider them vulgar—if colorful—relatives of the Big Three, pseudo-dragons are nonetheless vital to the ecology and people of their domains. Fierce and friendly, creatures of water, earth, air, and fire, each is a unique gem in the universe deserving our respect and protection. Such a motley crew creates a real cat-at-the-aquarium scenario for the average dracophile. Where does the feast begin? Alphabetically with an angelfish? Or perhaps by size with a guppy? It is a subjective process, at best. Since the vast numbers and types of pseudo-dragons make a comprehensive survey impractical in this allotted space, we present you, perforce, with a handful of eclectic (if unabashedly personal) favorites.

The Familiar:
Wyverns, Fire Drakes, and Lake Dragons

The most familiar pseudo-dragons are, naturally, those superficially most like True Dragons, particularly the Occidentals: wyverns, fire drakes, and lake dragons.

Wyverns

Large and winged, wyverns aloft are easily mistaken for Westies. On the ground, however, the physical differences are glaringly apparent: they average only about 6 meters (18–20 feet) in length, and, most notably, they do not have forelegs. Wyvern leathery wings sport bat-like claws for tearing prey, and their powerful legs can grasp or dismember most anything. But sure as nagas (cobra-esque pseudo-dragons from Asia) spread their hoods, they are bipedals and, thus, pseudo-dragons. This has not prevented wyverns from standing in for Dragons in art and tale, particularly as the victims of crusading saints who would have, in all likelihood, failed miserably against a proper Dragon.

Native to the European highlands and remote parts of Siberia from the northern Ural Mountains east to the Bering Sea, wyverns are loners by nature. Sexually mature individuals find each other for spring coupling, then the male goes his own way even before the female lays her eggs. Far from being a doting parent, the female buries her brood of three to six eggs and takes off, leaving the next generation to hatch and make it in the world as best they can. This throws young wyverns into a dragon-eat-dragon environment from the get-go, serving to both limit their numbers and hone their survival skills to an inevitably aggressive degree. Their martial dispositions have cast them as emblems of war, pestilence, and greed; on the flip-side, they can represent strength, bravery, and perseverance, qualities the nobles hoped to acquire when they placed this dragon on their family crests.

Though combative when pushed, wyverns are big-brained enough to know when discretion trumps battle. To that end, they frequently use their forest-toned scales to merge into their surroundings and quietly live to fly another day. When it comes to fighting, reports of wyverns breathing fire are hybridized fabrications at best. They do, however, pack wicked poison in their fangs and have been known to atomize it into a cloud that can stop a small army in their tracks.

Fire Drakes

Fire drakes (aka draks or drachs, depending on locale and linguistic variations), on the other hand, live up to their names and, when threatened, do not hesitate to employ a scorched-earth policy across great swaths the length and breadth of their lumbering bodies. While an effective self-defense, this indiscriminate approach has its drawbacks. Marsh drakes, for example, have been known to spark environmental disasters by setting the neighboring peat bogs on fire. They may have created a temporary buffer zone, but the cost in air quality and lost wetlands is considerable. Needless to say, fire drakes are not the brightest beings with scales: more brawn, less brain, but with very fine family instincts.

Drakes fall into the medium-large category of pseudo-dragon, reaching approximately 10 meters (33 feet) from tip to tail and looking for all intents and purposes like rotund Westies without wings—a definite pseudo giveaway. They live in caves—both natural and self-excavated—and are found throughout Europe, Asia, the Americas, and even parts of Africa. This expansive range has put them in the path of Homo sapiens since prehistoric times. As minerals for tools and status became an integral part of human existence, our ancestors found it more convenient to dislodge drakes from their metal-rich abodes than to dig new mines for themselves, resulting in one of the more common bits of hording lore. As with most errors in Dragon Studies, this myth speaks more to our nature than to theirs. The drakes were concerned with their creature comforts, not the iron or gold veining their cave walls. We were evicting them from their homes—homes they may have inhabited for generations. Conflict was inevitable. However, turnabout being fair play, during the last century drakes have been known to take up residence in mines we have exhausted. (The draconic views on strip mining can only be imagined!) This should be remembered when exploring seemingly abandoned caves and mines, especially during hatching season.

Which brings us to drake encounters in the wild.

As a rule, drake temperaments match their solid, rather ungainly physiques. Unable to fly to safety or even run with much dexterity, they prefer to hide or bluff their way out of dicey situations with bellows and unfurled neck frills that would scare off all but the most obstinate foe. They are slow to anger, yet they will not hesitate to use fire, tooth, and talon to great effect if protecting their family. So, when hiking through drake territory, keep your eyes open and give them the wide berth they deserve.

Lake Dragons

In the present, as in the past, water species comprise the most extensive family of pseudo-dragons. This is to be expected given that the planet itself is over 70 percent water. (Granted, only 3 percent of that is fresh, a fact that, while seriously impacting the nature and proliferation of mundane species, has not proved restrictive to dragons.) From mountain tarns to lowland bayous, lake dragons are found everywhere except Antarctica. Some are familiar, even famous: Scotland's Morag and the Loch Ness Monster, Vermont's Champ (Tatosok to the Abenaki tribe), Ogopogo from Lake Okanagan in British Columbia, Brosnya of Lake Brosno in Russia, Turkey's Van Lake Monster, and Mokèlé-mbèmbé of the Congo River. Known as knuckers, kelpies, mishipizhiws, and generic water serpents, they have inspired fear and wonder through the ages, and today they fill coffers with the tourist cash of the curious.

Though they are the most situationally diverse of the pseudo species, many a lay dracophile will insist that all lake dragons look pretty much alike from a distance. This is a cursory appraisal at best. True, they generally pass for Western/Eastern Dragon hybrids with supple, almost serpentine bodies (the better to swim with), long necks—which have led larger lake dragons to be mistaken for plesiosaurs (absurd! everyone knows plesiosaurs have been extinct for millions of years)—and ornately horned heads. They have broad chests to accommodate their big diver's lungs, webbed paws, and flat tails that spirit them through the waters. And while their long bodies and lack of wings clearly distinguish them as pseudo-dragons, beyond that, each breed is the distinctive product of their immediate environment. This plays itself out in a variety of ways, the most obvious being size. Like the proverbial goldfish, a water dragon's enormity is directly proportionate to that of the lake or river she calls home. It is an ecosystem no-brainer: expansive waterways not only provide room for growth, but also extensive buffets to please dragon (and Dragon) tastes. A pond dragon with only minnows and frogs on the menu—maybe the occasional newt or mudpuppy—will reach 2 meters (6.5 feet), tops; the crypto-residents of Lake Superior will be easily ten times that size.

Water dragons are adaptable to climate as well as habitat. In regions kissed by meteorological extremes, smaller, landlocked individuals settle down in the thick silt and drift into a dormant state from Winter Solstice to spring thaw. If caverns are handy, some dragons have been known to use them as hibernation chambers for the duration, though such terrestrial abodes can leave them vulnerable to people and the elements. Nessie, Champ, and their ilk, with their massive size and access to the sea, display a different sort of adaptability altogether: they migrate. Like bull sharks, they can alternate between freshwater and saltwater, their kidneys adjusting to the excess saline and filtering it from their systems. At the first touch of frost, these lake dragons head for the ocean, traveling southward along the subtropical currents to warmer climes (northward in the Southern Hemisphere). In essence, they become seasonal sea serpents, filling their bellies on rich ocean fare. From November to March, for example, the Sargasso Sea in the middle of the North Atlantic teems with dragons from Europe and the Americas, stuffing their maws on baby eels and young marlins and refreshing themselves in the nitrogen-rich waters. Come spring, they make the return trip to their freshwater homes to procreate and bask in the temperate summer sun. Unlike all True Dragons and most of their pseudo kin, water dragons from harsher climes have been known to be ovoviviparous, retaining their two or three eggs inside their bodies and, when circumstances are favorable, giving birth to live, well-developed young.

Undisturbed, water dragons tend to be free-spirited, even playfully disposed. Though this outward demeanor may remind the casual observer of dolphins frolicking in the surf, such an assessment is delusive, even reckless. Remember: even the most innocuous pseudo-dragon is still wild. Size and appetites must be taken into consideration, particularly if swimming or boating in their habitat without proper introduction or regard. The company of humans frequently inspires a more bashful, even defensive posture, but this is not always the case. The modern world's ecological shortsightedness is doing great harm to the relations between our species. We've disturbed their lives with motorboats and toxic petrochemicals; we've polluted and overfished their once-pristine hunting grounds, forcing them to find alternative food sources, to view livestock and even unescorted pets as suitable fare.

By driving formerly contented creatures out of their comfort zones and into ours, we have made battle lines inevitable. It is, after all, human nature to displace our woes whenever possible. One poor fishing season and local river dragons are transformed from benevolent totems into insatiable monsters; one missing poodle and we retaliate, puffed up with righteous indignation. Pitchforks and torches in hand, we persecute lake dragons for simply doing what any predator would to survive. Not to diminish the affection any of us hold for our companion animals, but one has only to look at the actions of our own kind *in extremis*—during famines (Jamestown in the Starving Time [1609–10], the Ukraine in the 1930s, China during the Great Leap Forward, to name but a few) or more singular disasters like those that befell the stranded Donner Party (1846–47) and the ill-fated Uruguay rugby team in the Andes (1972). Beneath scales, fur, or skin, instincts for self-preservation run deep in us all.

Today, increasingly rare though it may be, the sight of these graceful swimmers cavorting through morning mists warms the cockles of cryptoherpetologists' hearts around the globe. Their presence—or lack thereof—reminds us that the world is not ours to do with as we wish; that the planet's biospheres hang in increasingly delicate balance. Lake dragon needs are simple: they neither take more than life requires nor trash their own environments. And, like Oriental Dragons, they're indicative of vibrant waters and healthy ecosystems capable of supporting not only their own kind but also a whole range of flora and fauna, from water bug and canvasback duck to human. We ought to bear this in mind when we move into an area and claim a crystal-clear, seemingly unpopulated lakeside for our recreation; we may well be invading the last refuge of the Mesabi mere dragon or the Acadian fen flapper. If situations were reversed and water dragons clambered out of the Thames to take up residence in the parks of central London, surely we would not be amused.

It took centuries for wyverns, drakes, and lake dragons to garner their counterfeit Dragon credentials, and, in the process, they wound up seriously muddying the scientific waters. Naturalists like Pliny the Elder (23–79 CE) of Rome and Konrad Gessner (1516–65) of Switzerland, as well as artistic masters of observation and anatomy like Leonardo da Vinci and Raphael (1483–1520) insisted their draconic portraits were accurate, though, more often than not, they simply slapped wings on a (large) lizard, frequently one suffering from glaring limb and size deficits.[15] They were also depicted as violent, solitary beings, an interpretation so far

---

15. Some might insist it's unfair to lump da Vinci in with the rest. His "Dragon Attacking a Lion" is quite worthy of his subject, even if the "Dragon" is a wyvern, and a small wyvern at that. See chapter 8 for a closer examination of Dragons in the arts.

from the truth about the Big Three as to be downright revisionist. Generations of diligent cryptoscientists have had to untangle the subsequent misconceptions and begin to set the record straight. Marvelous as the creatures are from historical and aesthetic perspectives, where might Dragon Studies be today if naturalists spent more time in the field, focusing their empirical abilities on the weyrs around them and less at the hearth, rapt in local fictions?

The Foreign:
Tree-Skimmers, Diggers, and House Dragons

Avagrah, bobbi-bobbi, musussu, gowrow, kaukas...

Enumerating the more exotic pseudo-dragons is a labor that would make Gilgamesh quake in his sandals and Hercules go all fetal and suck his thumb. So we won't even try. Rather, we'll look at three of the more intriguing classes—tree-skimmers, diggers, and house dragons—and trust that your own curiosity will lead you to delve further.

Tree-Skimmers

Tree-skimmers are a family of small to medium-sized dragons presumed to be offshoots of the proto-dragons who survived the Triassic–Jurassic Extinction 200 million years ago and took to the trees for safety and snacks. Found in broad-leaf, old-growth forests from temperate zones to the tropics, they seldom (if ever) descend to the forest floor. And why should they when everything from roosts to nuts is right at their wingtips? Indeed, taking full advantage of their environment, tree-skimmers tend to be far more omnivorous than other pseudo-dragons. This only makes sense when surrounded by fresh fruits and vegetables.

Like small Feathered Dragons sans feathers, tree-skimmers use their slight size to maneuver through the trees, nesting and hunting without fear of breaking the branches beneath them. Also like Feathered Dragons, they use venom in place of fire, the latter being inadvisable in their surroundings. The height at which they live gives tree-skimmers the option of being gliders as well as active fliers. This makes them among the stealthiest of pseudo-dragons, ambushing their prey with a silent swoop from above. It also makes them dangerous to trespassers, particularly those with two legs and lumber on their minds. The New Guinea ropen, East African iaculus, and others of their ilk are infamous for blitzing the unsuspecting with poison-laced fangs and sabersharp claws.

The loss of mature forests and their inhabitants is the greatest threat to tree-skimmer existence. As real jungles give way to urban jungles, the more resilient species have found ways to adapt. Like the peregrine falcons, owls, and even eagles and vultures that have traded rocky aeries for glass-and-steel retreats and unruly wilderness for manicured parks, modern tree-skimmers have become positively cosmopolitan. Including such protein sources as rats, pigeons, squirrels, and (in harbor sites) gulls, they join birds of prey in keeping the numbers of those we consider vermin in check. Finding essential greens is more difficult. Availing themselves of human wastefulness, these pseudo-dragons will go dumpster-diving around supermarkets and restaurants as the need arises. More brazen individuals have been known to make aerial attacks on fruit stands and farmers' markets, picking off choice bok choy or muskmelons and vanishing in a flash. *Note:* The need for an omnivorous diet is a sure sign you're dealing with tree-skimmers, not garden-variety raptors; like strictly carnivorous pseudo-dragons, hawks, owls, and the like have a less-developed intestinal system, making them unable to properly digest plant matter. Instead, they extract essential vitamins and minerals directly from their prey, no veggies required.

Urban dracophiles intent on spotting tree-skimmers would do well to get a good pair of binoculars and look up, particularly in the great cities of Europe with their mighty Gothic cathedrals and palaces. Perched among granite gargoyles, they will sit for hours, camouflaged from all but the most discerning eye. In New World metropolises, with their hard-edged skyscrapers, the dragons are considerably more conspicuous. They must count on human ignorance to let them pass for large avians or even fruit bats in the right climate. In the United States, remnants of the nineteenth century's Gothic Revival provide welcome, if rare, havens. Visitors to New York should cast an eye around St. Patrick's Cathedral and the Cloisters, as well as in the wilder parts of Central Park. Landmarks such as Toronto's Casa Loma and Saint-Joseph's Oratory in Montreal are also hospitable habitats for urban tree-skimmers.

Diggers

From the treetops we descend to the subterranean world of the dragons known collectively as diggers. Footless to four-footed, low-slung, solid, powerful, and (as a rule) wingless, diggers are found in warmer, more arid climes, where they are frequently mistaken for (very) large monitor lizards.

This can prove a real danger for amateur naturalists: while monitors are mildly venomous and can deliver a nasty bite, they are seldom fatal to human beings. The same cannot be said of digger dragons, many of whom, like India's Golkonda gota (a spiny digger who enjoys hanging around diamond mines) and the Chilean copperback (a razor-scaled dragon who gets his name from rolling in the copper-rich dust of the Andes), not only sport toxins in their bite but also on quill tips, frills, spurs, and fine-edged scales.

As a class, diggers are the most ill-used of the pseudo-dragons, their story going paw-in-glove with that of the 3Ms: mankind, minerals, and mining. With talons slicing through bedrock like butter, the dragons dug tunnels deep underground—the largest of them tall enough for a person to wander through without so much as a crouch—exposing veins of ore and lodes of gems. To the uninformed and greedy, it looked as if the diggers, like their more imposing True Dragon kin, were not only collecting riches but actually dwelling in jewel-encrusted abodes. One thing led to another, and in no time at all these simple, modest creatures became fabled hoarders with treasure troves sure to make Blackbeard weep with envy. They were assumed, like people, to place a priority on such material goods, defending them with deadly intensity. Despite the error at its core, this hypothesis soon became part of the draconic canon. Of course, as any cryptoherpetologist will tell you, sparklies contribute to a burrow's décor but are hardly worth risking life and limb for, not even the vast collections amassed by Westies. The fact is that while certain precious metals and stones are excellent conductors of heat and thus fine nesting materials, for a Queen of any species, nothing is more important than the well-being of her eggs. These are the true treasure. Diggers are among the more aggressive dragons, but their behavior is a result of guarding families—not fortunes. Since we've been plundering their homes for millennia, a hostile reception is no less than we deserve.

Since Neolithic times, canny digger watching has been a sure route to riches that even modern metal detectors and radiographs can't outdo. Copper and iron for tools; gold, silver, and colorful crystals for currency and status—digger burrows held treasures our ancestors could not even imagine. Timna ouroboros, once abundant in Israel between the Dead Sea and the Gulf of Aqaba, were instrumental to King Solomon's mining operations; Yowah growlers unearthed mounds of opals in Australia; and lindworm trails from Uzbekistan to South Africa have led people to jade, diamonds, rainbows of precious beryl, and, of recent interest, promethium, thorium, and other rare elements.

As our worlds became more and more enmeshed, confrontations became furious and inevitable. Mutually devastating at first, with sorry irony that runs through the history of Dragon/human relationships, these battles soon tipped in mankind's favor thanks to weapons constructed from the very metals discovered in dragon (and Dragon) dens. The situation got worse with the rise of Western monotheism. With Dragons and their cousin species coming under attack as fiery creatures in Satan's service, it did not help the diggers to literally emerge from the Underworld. Spindleston wyrms and Highland beithirs, Etruscan basilisks, and the sugaar of the Andorran hills—not one escaped such wicked associations. In the name of saving souls, religious powers enlisted dragon slayers by the score and enriched their coffers on the broken backs of creatures simply trying to survive.

The largest of the diggers are gone now, victims of urban expansion and modern mining methods. It was impossible for them to survive when we blew the tops off their mountains and stripped the land bare. Smaller species can still be found, often taking up residence in mine shafts once theirs, then ours, now theirs again—a cosmic cycle. In the U.K., for example, abandoned tin mines are particular favorites of the Cornish Tyr druics—earth dragons. These stubby-legged bipedal diggers are 3 meters long (10 feet) with trace winglets, spade-shaped tails, and snout and mental scales modified into hard beaks. Taken as the sum of their parts, they're as effective as backhoes for moving through rock and soil. Every now and then, when the night sky allows, they can be spotted ambling across Cornwall's Bodmin Moor, eyes ashimmer with moonshine.

As any cryptohistorian can tell you, humans owe these terrestrial prowlers a great debt, one which we have fallen far short in repaying. That they have not taken us to task for our negligence speaks volumes about their natures. Still, use due diligence when exploring caves and old shafts, and keep a discreet distance from *any* digger you espy. They are understandably skittish and even the smallest one can take off an intrusive limb with ease.

House Dragons

Virtually every culture has its species of *Draco domesticus*, from the frilled walek of the Australian outback to the fiery-tailed kaukas of Lithuania. Seldom more than a meter (3 feet) in length, these nimble globetrotters are the toy breeds of the pseudo-dragon world, snuggling up close to human habitations, bringing good fortune to those who treat them well and travesty to those who treat them ill.

The code of house-dragon husbandry is simple: provide them with shelter, warmth, daily meals, and the occasional scratch on the tummy, and you will garner their lifelong loyalty and protection. They will control rodents and other intrusive pests and even keep unwanted solicitors and bill collectors at bay. Some of the more sociable species are particularly adept at watching children, though it is essential to teach your kids proper dragon safety. Dragon ivories are sharp, and some will breathe fire or spit venom if threatened. Terrible though this sounds, remember that dogs and cats do not hesitate to use their teeth and claws, and a parrot's beak can slice a hand down to the bone, yet these are everyday domestic companions. Though they choose to be close to hearth and family, house dragons are still wild creatures and need to be treated with due deference. We're talking Dragon Interaction 101: Don't pull their wings or step on their tails, and never to put your fingers near their mouths before they've eaten breakfast. These are simple rules but particularly important for children to know inside-out. With a little preparatory work, you can avoid distressing your dragon and/or making unwanted trips to the emergency room.

Among the most democratic of species, house dragons appreciate kindness from any source regardless of social standing. In fact, they are more apt to put down roots with modest farming families than with royals. The reasons for this behavior are anyone's guess—basic opportunity springs to mind, peasants being more numerous than aristocrats—though, in our tendency to give dragons human qualities, we like to think they recognize that a gift of milk or eggs—even grain—means the most coming from those who can afford it least. It is quite possible they simply prefer the freedom and simplicity of rural living to the confines of court and the demands of the rich and powerful.

The larger of the house dragons, like the musussu of ancient Babylon, stand in opposition to this precept. Descendants of the great Dragon Sirrush, musussu were guards of the royal palace and Ishtar's Gate. Unfortunately, the constant turmoil in the Middle East has driven the last of their kind underground, making it impractical to chart their modern habits; impossible to know if, left to their own devices, they would choose to continue their urban existence or move out to the windswept wilds.

Central to house dragon lore are tales of their generosity, specifically the blessing of their people with material goods—coins, gems, and precious nuggets. Some, like the Lithuanian smij, provide more practical goods: a granary full of corn from the zitny smij, a goodwife's dairy aflood with milk from the mlokowy smij. In the past, all such windfalls—especially the monetary ones—were attributed to magic and, consequently, captured the unwanted attention of alchemists. Today we know the truth is far simpler: prowling at night, they pick up brilliant objects that catch their eye. Then, like a proud tabby with a mouse, they deposit them on the bed and wait for you to admire their prowess. While this is a blessing for the recipient, one family's gain is necessarily another's loss. In parts of the world where house dragons are plentiful, this can—and has—lead to long-term civil strife. Over time, such feuds influence the surrounding lore, often changing the very nature of the local species from good to ill depending on who is telling the tale. Gargoyles are a clear case in point. Related to but not to be mistaken for Gargouille—the water-spouting Seine River creature slain by St. Romanus (c. 641 CE)—these nocturnal, often eccentric creatures are affectionately known as the pit bulls of the house dragons. They gravitate to *chateaux* and *maisons de champagne* throughout Western Europe, acting as superb watchdragons for court and vineyard. Territorial in the extreme, they have been known to lay waste to rival lands at the urging of their particular humans. Such actions led to bloody gargoyle wars and resulted in them being cast as dark, violent beings who would eat you as soon as look at you.

None of this is true. Well, almost none.

As with mundane species, the problem lies not with the dragons but with their people. Encouraged to snarl rather than purr, boundaries and socialization skills fall by the wayside, and they turn from boon to bane in the twitch of a griffin's tail. During the fifteenth and sixteenth centuries, the French guardians were considered too dangerous to be kept, setting off a nationwide eradication program that spilled over onto even the most benign of species. By the time Louis XIV took the throne in 1643, gargoyles were practically unknown save in a handful of aristocratic households. The French Revolution, with its violently anti-royalist sentiments, sent even those few dragons to rout, both the democratic Jacobin party and the republican Girondists preferring their gargoyles set in stone atop cathedrals.

Thanks to our improved understanding of dragon behavior, these faithful watchers are finally receiving the appreciation they so richly deserve. Over the last half century their numbers in Europe and the Americas have been on the rise, aided by the fact that they're one of the rare pseudo species as comfortable in the city as the country. In fact, they have adapted so well to the post-Industrial world as to be positively urbanized. If we continue working with their strengths rather than bending them to our desires, we can look forward to a long, mutually beneficial coexistence with house dragons.

The study of pseudo-dragons is wide open and in need of curious, hard-working field researchers. For those interested in spending time with the rich array of these creatures, a few parting words of wisdom:

1. **Know your environment.** Always have an emergency exit planned. Given our limited knowledge of these dragons, particularly the rarer venomous species, timely access to the nearest hospital can be crucial.

2. **Know your species.** Remember the lesson of the tiny yet deadly blue-ringed octopus: Hazard is not always proportionate to size.

3. **Look, don't touch.** Some species, such as the bipedal aspis, are as dangerous with a scale cut as with a bite.

4. **Keep a fully charged cell phone with you at all times.** Put emergency numbers on speed dial. This gadget of the modern world has been a real gift to field workers.

5. **Have a good camera with a zoom lens and lots of memory cards or film.** High-speed

Ektachrome film is the stock of choice among
many professionals. Even in this digital age,
there are times when only a classic will do.

That said, just step back, give the pseudo-dragons their
space, and, to the best of your ability, safeguard their tenu-
ous place in the modern world.

Part II

Dragons in Faith, Magic, and the Arts

Dragons in Religion and Philosophy

Dragons have no need for religion. Understand that from the start.

Leaving the heavy lifting of the Creation behind them, Dragons stepped out of myth, shedding much their divine luster in the process. And that was fine with them. It's hard enough to survive in the world without having to live up to the expectations of others. But we would not let them go. For good and ill, we needed Dragons as pillars of our faiths. Across seven seas, from desert sands to glacial peaks, we drew them into our human belief systems, demanding they play integral roles—literal and symbolic, sacred and profane—in our battle with the infinite. True to our modern views on Dragons, in the East, they were our allies; in the West, they ultimately became our foes.

Asian Faith, Philosophy, and Dragons

There is a *koan* (Zen saying) whispered in the enchantments of Shikoku, Japan: What is the shape of God's breath? It is the Dragon, sleeping!

From the Indus River in Pakistan to the Pacific Ocean, Asian Dragons have been an honored part of the spiritual scheme of things for thousands of years. In the early days, they were tribal guardians and shamanic advisors. Then they consorted with gods and sages, pulled Yu the Great's (c. 2200–2100 BCE) chariot across the heavens, and were tamed by Buddha (c. 563–483 BCE). Nearly every village had its Dragon shrine, where anthems were offered for luck, wisdom, and plentiful rains. In short, Dragons were as much a part of daily life and belief as breathing.

When tribes became nations, civilization began to give structure to the chaotic. The legendary Fu Hsi (c. 2900 BCE) is considered by many to be the father of this cultural transformation. He was the survivor of the Great Flood, forebear of the Chinese people, inventor of writing, religion, fishing, and the *I Ching* (or *Book of Changes*), the book of wisdom and divination consulted on everything from diplomacy and war craft to domestic living. According to the historian Ban Gu (32–92 CE),

> *he looked upward and contemplated the images in the heavens, and looked downward and contemplated the occurrences on earth. He united man and wife, regulated the five stages of change, and laid down the laws of humanity.*[16]

---

16. *I Ching*, 329.

And he was part Dragon, to boot!

So it was from the beginning that the enchantments of China were caught in the midst of these swirling currents of change. As naturally as shedding their skin, Dragons transitioned through the centuries from the simple faith of folkways to the heart of Asian mysticism and philosophy. By the Age of the Three Sovereigns (2800 BCE) their powerful essence of action and balance was immortalized in the newly penned text and commentaries of the *I Ching*.[17] There they continued to hold sway through the spiritual heyday of King Wen (1099–1056 BCE), founder of the Zhou Dynasty (1046–256 BCE), on to the more pragmatic approach of Confucius (551–479 BCE).

In his commentaries, *Shi Yi* (*The Ten Wings*), Confucius turned the *I Ching*'s spiritualism into a teaching tool for those who would be wise leaders concerned with the public good. This was a beneficial approach to a world full of war lords and tribal infighting, yet too strict a code of conduct to appeal to the region's Dragons. They would not be constrained as symbols of moral living and political leadership, no matter how high minded. Like the more rigid qualities of the Greek philosophers Socrates and Aristotle, the straitjacket of fifth-century BCE ethics was for beings living outside the cosmic way; beings in whom the forces of yang and yin—masculine and feminine, active and passive—were in conflict. Dragons are creatures so natural and complete that such conflict is completely foreign to them. (The perfection of Dragons applies to all True species, though in the West

---

17. Ibid., 3–10.

they've had a much harder time convincing people of this fact.) In the Spring and Autumn Period of Chinese history (722–476 BCE), they were simply waiting for the rest of the world to catch up with them.

They were waiting for Laozi. Some consider Laozi a contemporary of Confucius, though their exact dates have been muddled through the years. Like Dragons, both men straddle legend and history; for our purposes we will place them somewhere around 500 BCE. Laozi's spiritual influence is in some places contemporaneous with Confucianism; in others, its successor.

Dragons, Taoism, and Buddhism

Confucius focused on the world within society and civic responsibility, but Laozi dove into the mysticism beyond society, the spiritual wisdom in the natural and spontaneous, and found the Tao.

As Laozi set down in the *Tao Te Ching*, the Tao is the inexplicable, fundamental Way of the Universe, the producer of the ten thousand things. Each thing has its own *te* (integrity) that sets it apart from all else. A thing's te is the distinctive combination of yin and yang, light and dark that preserves its place in the Universe.

> *All beings support* yin *and embrace* yang
> *and the interplay of these two forces*
> *fills the universe.*
> *Yet only at the still-point,*
> *between the breathing in and the breathing out,*
> *can one capture these two in perfect harmony.*[18]

---

18. Lao Tzu and Star, *Tao Te Ching: Definitive Edition*, 55.

This is Dragon territory.

Interestingly, the word *lung* (Dragon) appears nowhere in the eighty-one verses of the *Tao Te Ching*. It doesn't have to. When Laozi looked into the sky, he saw Dragons dancing among the clouds. They were impulsive and wild. They knew how to get out of their own way, to live in the still-point. Mercurial and eternal, appearing then vanishing, they effortlessly embraced their place in the universe. In Dragons, Laozi saw balance, motion, and harmony as in no other creature on Earth. To mention them by name would only serve to set them apart, to remove them from the Way.

Dragons did not need to learn the Tao. They *were* the Tao.

As Japanese scholar Okakura Kakuzo (1862–1913) explained in *The Book of Tea*:

> *The Tao is in the Passage rather than the Path. It is the spirit of Cosmic Change,—the eternal growth which returns upon itself to produce new forms. It recoils upon itself like the dragon... It folds and unfolds as do the clouds... Subjectively it is the Mood of the Universe. Its Absolute is the Relative.*[19]

Nothing is as absolutely relative as a Dragon.

In ways more metaphysical than religious, Taoism and the Dragons who symbolize it were adaptable to the spiritual winds blowing through Eastern Asia. When Mahayana Buddhism spread out of India into China's Han Empire in the first century CE, the Eight-Fold Path found many parallels with the Way. Living in accord with the Tao was not dissimilar to tapping into one's Buddha nature. In an

---

19. *The Book of Tea*, 12.

effort to make converts, it was only natural for the Buddhist missionaries to take their tales and images of the Indian dragon—or *naga*—and translate them into those of the Chinese *lung*; to build their monasteries and convents, as religious historian J. J. M. de Groot (1854–1921) notes,

> *in mountains where dragons caused thunderstorms and tempests, floods and inundations, with the object of bridling these imaginary beasts; or where, on the contrary, monks had conjured away droughts by compelling dragons to send down their rains...*[20]

Leading up to this, the naga had already undergone a fierce transformation from the vast snakelike creature of Hindu scriptures (aka Vedas) that was constantly at war with gods and men to the benevolent being reformed through the grace of the Buddha's gaze. According to legend, Gautama was meditating under the Bodhi tree when a great storm rose up. King Naga Muchalinda emerged from his underground lair and spread his great hood over the Enlightened One, protecting him from the elements for seven days and nights. For this kindness, Muchalinda and his kin were blessed as the first of the animals to touch their Buddha nature. (In the eternal fluidity of the draconic world, who's to say that Buddha didn't use the time with Muchalinda to get in touch with his Dragon nature?) According to oral tradition and Buddhist texts (*sutras*), naga anger that caused the heavens to storm became the generous harbinger of rain for the parched land,[21] and the

---

20. Groot, *The Religion of the Chinese*, 186. As scholarly as de Groot was, his perspective on Dragons as imaginary is clearly the product of early-twentieth-century European bias.

21. Visser, *Dragon in China and Japan*, 25–27.

gem they guarded from all comers became the pearl of wisdom and good fortune. In anticipation of Buddhism's global reach, they were metamorphosing into beings recognizable from one end of the continent to another.

Traveling east in the Buddha's entourage, these newly exalted nagas shed their more cobra-esque traits for the classical aspect of the local Dragons. They traded hoods for manes and sprouted legs. Like the indigenous lung, they were split into four essential classes: heavenly, divine, earthly, and hidden (according to Zen tradition, there is a fifth class, the coiled Dragon, who lives in the sea and cannot yet rise to heaven); four physical classes: scaled, winged, horned, and unhorned; and four colored classes: red, white, green, and blue (the still semi-divine azure and yellow Dragons remained beyond the shifting pale). Skeptics suggest that some of these changes were merely cosmetic, a savvy ploy by which the Mahayana monks sought to connect with the people of China, aka the Children of the Dragon. If so, it worked. Not only did the Buddhist Dragons mesh neatly with those of Chinese fact and lore, but, logically, the emperor cast a friendlier eye upon any foreigners who shared his affection for the great creatures.

Over the centuries, the teachings of Buddha intermingled with those of Laozi (and even Confucius) and moved through Korea and across the sea to Japan, going all Zen in the process. The Dragons of Asia were embraced by one and all with a stylistic consistency that, far from being coincidental, speaks to a deep-seated, global sense of Dragons. From form to habits, the region's Dragons were similar enough to move between one belief system and another without shedding a single scale of their integrity. They were Tao and te to the bone.

The Dragon's Pearl

Still, for many, Dragons were moving out of the literal realm into the symbolic. Image was everything, whether or not it was understood, and one of the least understood images in sacred Dragon iconography is that of their precious pearl. It's said there are as many interpretations of the Dragon's gem as there are poisonous *fugu* (blowfish) in the sea. While no doubt a generous overstatement from some daredevil sushi lover, as with most things Dragon, there is more than a dash of truth here.

Like the Dragon herself, the orb in her possession has transformed with locale, time, and religious traditions, dancing between a fiery sphere shot through with lightning and the most perfect pearl ever coughed up by the sea. According to Hindu traditions, the naga-maids who lived under the sea were draped in strings of pearls of good fortune. Among Buddhists, this became known as the divine pearl—or *cintamani* stone—granter of all desires.[22] In Tibet it represented the sun, which the Cosmic Dragon stalked, caught, and swallowed (or at least tried to). This not only gave her a wicked case of heartburn but also fiery breath. In *The Dragon in China and Japan*, M. W. de Visser suggests it might as easily be the moon they're pursuing; not only is the moon associated with water and rain but "having been swallowed by the dragon, might have been believed to strengthen the rain-giving power of the latter."[23] And, in

---

22. In the global draconic scheme of things, this relates closely to the Philosopher's Stone of the West, over which alchemists and Dragons wrestled for centuries. See chapter 7.

23. Visser, *Dragon in China and Japan*, 106.

ancient Japan, where the people counted on the benevolent swells of the oceans, the gem stood for the lustrous tidal jewel the Dragon King Ryu-jin held in his paws. He gave this pearl to his son-in-law, Hoori, so that he might control the tides for humanity's sake.

But nowhere is the symbology of the orb more elaborate than in China. Stories dating back to prehistoric times insist it is a Dragon's egg, tucked close under the Queen's chin. The egg produces not only a little Dragonlet but also thunderous roars befitting the ruler of the river, rain, and sea. What else would a Dragon hold so dear? This pearl-as-egg theory led generations of cryptoherpetologists to mistakenly assume that Asian Dragons lived outside of the traditional weyr/enchantment social structure. They were thought to be footloose rogues, laying one egg at a time, with Queens remaining alone and virtually on-wing for the whole incubation period. As we now know, though Eastern clutches are small, the rest of this scenario is fancy.

There is a variation on the thunder-rain motif known as the Wall of the Nine Dragons theory, in reference to a wall in Beijing's Forbidden City. As the name implies, the wall shows nine Dragons, each with spheres dancing just beyond their reach, crackling with ribbons of lightning and marked by a commalike spiral that cuts to the orb's core. Scholars have insisted this represents the unbridled power of Dragons as thunder gods. (It also looks remarkably like the *lung zhu guo*—Dragon pearl fruit—a treat packed with healthy qualities. But I digress.)

While the lightning—shaped like a Dragon's horns— is relatively obvious, the meaning of the comma shape has been disputed through the ages. Traditional priests of the Wu

Kingdom in the fifth century BCE believed the whirl symbolized the rolling thunder at the heart of the storm. Using charms and shrines, they sought to tap the power of Dragons and their orbs to ensure fertile rains and bountiful harvests. Of course, when religious changes swept the region, this notion, like Dragons themselves, was open to adaptation.

Confucius and his disciples were influenced by trends trickling across the Himalayas and down the Silk Road and thus saw the swirl as the fiery life energy within the jewel of worldly desires. This no doubt stemmed from a Stone Age belief in Dragon's all-consuming passion for sparklies intermingled with a growing disdain for the old folk faiths. There is a tale from the time of a follower of Confucius, T'an-t'ai Mieh-ming, who ran afoul of the god of the Huang He River. With divine urging, a pair of Dragons rose out of the water and ambushed the fellow on pretext of robbing him of a rare and magical gem. T'an-t'ai dispatched the Dragons and then, in an act of self-righteous bravado, tossed the stone into the river. "I have no need for such worldly things!" he cried. But the river, mourning the loss of her Dragons, would have none of it and spit the stone back. Twice, the man cast it away and twice the Huang He returned it. Finally, he shattered the gem into a thousand pieces and scattered the bits far and wide. As you might imagine, this story does not set well with Dragons. If T'an-t'ai was going to get rid of the stone anyway, why did he kill the Dragons? Why not simply give it them? Ah, but that would have benefited the folksy river god. And the Dragons. Is it any wonder our whiskered friends preferred the Taoists over Confucianists?

Fortunately, some Confucianists—and many Taoists of the day—looked deeper and saw the whirl as the smoky mark of Dragon wisdom, rare and priceless.

During the Tang Dynasty (600–900 CE), Buddhism—particularly Zen Buddhism—converged with a major Taoist revival. Throughout Eastern Asia, Dragons were regarded as the blessed Keepers of the Way. The squiggle on their pearl was seen as the curl dividing yin and yang and was thus symbolic of the Tao. This popular misconception was bolstered by figurative kinship with the *tomoe* of Japan. Found in Buddhist and Shinto shrines across Japan, often two- or three-fold (*fatatsu-domoe* or *mitsu-domoe*), the commalike *tomoe* swirl is a sign of Cosmic unity and the eternal cycle of life, both things Dragons understand very well. When viewed in conjunction with similar solar spirals around the globe—the Celtic triskelions spring to mind—its potential meanings expand exponentially: light, sun, power, truth, wisdom, birth, rebirth, life, the universe, and everything.

One of the most fascinating and potent takes on the swirl-in-the-pearl is actually more biological than theological. A familiar image in Chinese silks and plaster shows two sinuous Dragons—one ascending, one descending—with the pearl dancing between them. It is alive with fire, plasma charges—the universal *qi*, or life force, begetter of all energy and creation. This taps into a cosmic understanding of the origins of life, presenting the Dragons as the double helix of DNA. The pearl becomes the first ovum (yin) invaded by the first sperm (yang)—divine or natural, depending on your point of view. This union ignited the primal ooze and made us all possible. While the thought of our ancient ancestors being mystically attuned to twentieth-century scientific discoveries may give you pause, it is worth remembering that "All greatness is improbable. What's probable is tedious and petty."[24]

The truth is, the pearl could be all these things or none of them. It's anyone's guess. Modern symbologists are inclined to come down on the side of thunder and lightning; it's the safe bet. The more adventurous find it interesting that, over the centuries, kings, poets, and sages have consorted with Dragons, yet no one has gotten a definitive answer on this matter. Granted, Dragons have as little use for symbols as for religion and may well have chosen, as a matter of draconic contradiction, to remain mum on the subject. This would not only increase their credentials as enigmas par excellence, but would also drive humans right up the wall. Enjoyable though this scenario might be, it is just as likely that the humans in their company never bothered to ask, attesting to our deplorable and frequent lack of curiosity. That said, anyone who has been privileged to see a Dragon juggling her pearl cannot help but feel the act of Creation playing out before their eyes.

Today, despite growing secularism, the position of Asian Dragons remains a deeply spiritual one. Their history is strong: From one end of Asia to another, they spent centuries embraced by every faith and philosophy the continent had to offer. They flirted with Buddhists, bureaucrats, emperors, and priests, each doing their best to lay claim to the draconic spirit. Modern orthodoxy be damned, the

---

24. Lao Tzu and Le Guin, *Tao Te Ching: A Book About the Way*, 86.

old ways retain enough clout among the people to assure Dragon tolerance at the very least.

And today, as in the past, the Dragon's heart flies closest to the Tao. Comfortable in their own skins, at one with the Universe, they epitomize the Tao attained.

> *Heaven (ch'ien) gives,*
> *and all things turn out for the best*
> *The Sage lives,*
> *and all things go as Tao goes*
> *all things move as the wind blows*[25]

"Watch us," they seem to say with a wink. "We are wind and rain; we rise to the heavens and ride the Way."

These are sacred Dragons at their best and most accessible. Those who hear them are attuned to the Tao. Those who see them are blessed by the Universe.

Western Faith and Dragons

For all their mystery, Eastern Dragons and the people who adore them have taught us one simple thing: the closer we are to the natural way of the Universe, the more at one we are with Dragons. Conversely, the further we stray from the path—especially its wilder, more spontaneous aspects—the more divided we are. This disconnect leads to fear and loathing and, in an eggshell, explains the woeful history of Dragons and Western religion. From the Stone Age to the present, Westies' shifting fortunes have run parallel with the demise of Paganism and the rise of monotheism.

---

25. Lao Tzu and Star, *Tao Te Ching: Definitive Edition*, 94.

Not that there weren't good times. Shaman and European Dragon once crossed paths on a regular basis, particularly in the North, where weyr residents were regarded with much the same esteem as their Eastern kindred. Together with tribal holy men, they romped along Earth's ley lines (energy grid) and haunted ritual caves, sacred pools, and groves. That the Dragons held rights of *primum cubilia*—first nesting—was never contested. They were old as the hills beneath their feet and that signified. In a society where age meant wisdom, they were the wisest beings around. Anyone who could claim draconic counsel was practically guaranteed a long and prosperous reign. And, as the top predators in a hunter-gatherer world, they not only commanded respect, their totemic blessings were coveted more than gold.

Sadly, when it comes to specifics of wisdom shared, bans on writing down sacred teachings have greatly handcuffed scholars. Oral histories and artifacts left a few clues, which in turn led to reasoned speculation—particularly with respect to the ancient Celts and Druids. But we're still guessing. As Western humanity slouched toward the Bronze Age (3600–600 BCE), draconic knowledge of metallurgy, warcraft, herbs, and crystal lore would have made them instrumental to the development of European civilization as we know it. It is also believed they torched wicker men and ritual pyres and taught the ancients the art of scrying in the still waters of forest pools.

What Dragons wouldn't have given for such simple times to endure! Unfortunately, human populations grew; we left hunting and gathering behind and moved to more farm-based lifestyles that could support the emerging towns and cities. In the process, conflicts over space and resources arose.

After all, it's hard to blame anyone—even Dragons—for choosing to dine on plump, penned sheep rather than flying oneself ragged in potentially fruitless hunts for sinewy mountain goats. Was this the anti-Dragon rallying point one might imagine? No. But, over time, it proved to be a wedge issue that paved the way for philosophical and theological changes to come. And those changes started in the Middle East.

Back in the Chalcolithic, or Copper, Age (c. 4000 BCE), the primitive peoples of the Near East and Caucasus Mountains of south-central Russia were transitioning between nomadic and settled, stone-tooled and metal. Within a millennium, the Fertile Crescent villages of Eridu, Ur, Lagash, and Susa blossomed into thriving city-states. It was a new era, one in which ziggurats—towering, manmade temples—replaced sacred sun-kissed peaks, and skin tents gave way to brick-and-wood abodes. Where the land itself was once divine, now a pantheon of strikingly human gods and goddesses cropped up to rule soil and sea, rains and winds, to civilize the wilderness and inspire the people to do the same. It was becoming a world more urban and politic, in which waters were diverted and Dragons displaced. The awe once felt watching Cosmic Dragons like Gandareva and Ophion stretch their wings beneath the heavens was transferred to faux deities fashioned by human hands and locked away in lamp-lit temples, separated from the universe they were meant to command.

The mere fact of cities was at odds with the natural order, and novice urbanites saw the world beyond city walls in malevolent opposition to their new way of life. It was a reasonable—if paranoid—leap of logic to view huge, natural Dragons as the embodiment of this looming danger.

The ancients looked to leaders who could keep such threats from their doors, who would risk all for civilization's sake. This was the field on which legendary dragon slayers like King Gilgamesh of Uruk, and Rustam, hero of Persian mythology, played. Despite noble, for-the-greater-good justifications, at the end of the day, their anti-Dragon deeds were all about control. A hero, whether self-appointed or touched by the Fates, can't take on the whole planet; but he might settle for a piece of it—a draconic piece. This provides an adrenaline-filled sense of control, temporary and false though it may be. The problem for Dragons comes when the rush fades and begs for an encore.

Thankfully, despite growing heroes' blood lust, not all the region's Dragons were killed; many were forced into what can only be called the first of numerous diaspora, leaving the fertile plains and coastal lands for craggy, less populated uplands and deserts.

Dragons in the Garden

During the second millennium BCE, how people thought about the Divine took another radical turn, abandoning remnants of complex, still vaguely nature-based polytheism[26] for simpler anthropomorphic monotheism. This was the time of prophets and patriarchs and the One God storming onto the Western stage with a booming voice and a capital G. This was a God who was omniscient, omnipotent,

---

26. The Egyptian pantheon was one of the last in the region rich with sacred animal/human hybrids, including Thoth/Ibis; Horus/Falcon; Anubis/Jackal; and Bastet/Cat. Like Dragons, these were complicated beings, combining the beauty and violence of the natural world without moral judgment.

omnificent—omni-everything. Guardians of specific locales (woods, peaks, and streams), be they draconic or otherwise, were not only extraneous but also at odds with the notion of such a Supreme Being. If there could be only one deity, then all other astonishing forces must either serve Him or stand against Him. In this increasingly black-and-white, us-versus-them environment, "them" were about to be turned into devils. Dragons were as "them" as they come.

The Garden of Eden is a case in point.

Long ago, when human beings still struggled with flint blades and bone needles, the Persian Gulf was a lush tract of land as large as Great Britain. There the One River branched into the Four—Pishon, Gihon, and the ever popular Tigris and Euphrates—and beasts of every kind were plentiful. The place was thick with Dragons. The descendants of the great Chaos Dragon, Tiamat, swam in the waters off the coast of Qeshm and basked in the golden sands where the day begins. They guarded the sweet waters and fruitful trees and kept the balance among flora and fauna. When humans moved into the neighborhood, the Dragons taught them the ways of the land, the names of the creatures, and so on. They showed them which plants gave life and which ones took it. As long as tree and river, mountain and sea were holy, all was well. In this primal grove the Dragons ruled with a benevolent paw.

This was Eden, figuratively and quite possibly—according to recent archaeological theory—literally. Then, around 6000 BCE, the level of the Indian Ocean rose and drowned the fertile lowland in an event both as catastrophic and as natural as Dragonfire.[27] While the local enchantments simply moved to higher ground, the lost humans fast became the stuff of legend, shaped and reshaped by the swirling winds of civilization.

One of the most revisionist takes on this lost paradise is found in the Book of Genesis, as set down by the followers of Yahweh. A hand-me-down tale, the Genesis narrative opens in the land of the Four Rivers with Yahweh celebrating his creative labors, smiling at the world's diversity: animals and plants, fish and fowl. And human beings. Yet unlike Pagan faiths that placed people within the broad fold of existence, this God set Adam and Eve—a vanity project made in the divine image—apart from the natural world, and gave them dominion over all. Thus, according to the Judeo-Christian tradition, they were God's proxies here on Earth. Belief in this anointed standing not only set off a battle royale among the heavenly hosts (the name Lucifer springs to mind), but in more recent times has led to human assaults on the planet that would make any parent, divine or otherwise, weep.

What happened to the Dragons, you ask?

The simple explanation is that they were transformed into reptilian agents of evil, most notably the silver-tongued

27. Of course, a happening of such magnitude was ripe for divine interpretation. In time, it was transformed into a deluge full of judgment and punishment. See *The Epic of Gilgamesh*, Tablet XI and the Bible, Genesis 7–9.

Serpent, "wisest of all creatures."[28] In one fell swoop, the duality essential to a monotheistic world was created: if the Creator was all good, then he/she must be balanced by some force that is all wicked. This also served to draw a line in the sand between the new faith of Yahweh and the old, Dragon-respecting ways. For a faith that insists "Thou shalt have no other gods before me," the Dragon/serpent-cum-devil was a convenient symbol of the ancient Pagans with their nature-loving ways. The enchantments that helped the early people of the Middle East were no longer on the "us" side of the divide, for "us" had been chosen by God, elevated from the rest of the animal world. This cast Dragons as "other" and fearfully alien, waiting to lure mankind away from the Divine One and back to the Demonic Many, all feral darkness and subtle temptation.

Eastern Dragons would laugh long and loud at the idea of subtlety being a bad thing. Indeed, were Westies not on the receiving end of such a curse, they'd likely join in the chortle. Truly, all True Dragons prize quick intelligence and complex wit; to do any less is considered a waste of talents,

---

28. *Nag Hammadi Library in English*, "On the Origin of the World" (New York: Harper & Row, 1988), 184. Unlike traditional Judeo-Christian texts, Gnostic writings were far more generous—almost Taoist—about Dragons, remarking frequently on their wisdom. See the Gospel of Thomas, 124–38. Those who insist that the Serpent was a snake, not a Dragon, would be advised to re-examine Genesis 3:14: "And the Lord God said unto the serpent, Because thou hast done this, thou art cursed above all cattle, and above every beast of the field; upon thy belly shalt thou go, and dust shalt thou eat all the days of thy life" (King James Bible). The implication is that prior to crossing God, the Serpent had legs like other creatures. Losing them was a divine punishment. There is no mention of wings, though as the concept of Satan develops, it is clear he sports draconic wings, at least in the artistic imagination.

not to mention an impediment to learning. It is only the shallow and incurious of the world—the sheep rather than the shepherds—who would deride such gifts.

The Dragons of Eden shared wisdom freely. It was in their nature. Unlike Yahweh, they were not worried about scrawny two-legged beings becoming their equals—they were Dragons, after all! The lessons they offered were not only essential for human survival but also organic and accessible. Yahweh, on the other hand, preferred to leave Adam and Eve in the dark. Before the Dragon/serpent interfered, ignorance in Eden was bliss; after that, Yahweh had to settle for a redefinition of terms: knowledge was the forbidden fruit, attained through temptation and, as such, a sin. We all know how well that turned out.

Daniel and the Dragon

Out of Eden, the position of the Dragon with regard to Western religion grew more and more precarious. Dragons and their friends—human and divine—were vulnerable wherever and whenever they were found, including among the hanging gardens and crystal canals of Babylon. Which brings us to the Hebrew Apocrypha and the tale of Daniel. The Apocrypha are a collection of scriptures, many of questionable origin, which were omitted from the standard Bible. One such text speaks of how the prophet Daniel not only survived a den full of hungry lions, but slew a sacred Dragon as well.

In the sixth century BCE, Babylon was quite the cosmopolitan place. People of different faiths and tribal affiliations mingled with relative peace, living and worshipping as they chose. Thanks to his ability to read dreams, Daniel, though a Jew, became a confidant and advisor of King Cyrus. One day, the king, unaware of the maxim "Friends should never discuss religion or politics," pressed Daniel on his beliefs, starting with why he worshiped Yahweh and not the local idol, Bel.

> *Because I may not worship idols made with hands, but the living God, …*
>
> *Then said the king unto him, Thinkest thou not that Bel is a living God? Seest thou not how much [offerings] he eateth and drinketh every day?*
>
> *Then Daniel smiled, and said, O king, be not deceived: for this is but clay within, and brass without, and did never eat or drink anything.*[29]

Once Cyrus conceded that Bel was an artifact rather than a deity, he asked Daniel what he thought of the Dragon worshipped and adored by the people. Though Daniel could not contest the living, breathing reality of the Dragon, he did question the Dragon's divinity, insisting that a creature's mortality made him unworthy of reverence:

> *Then said Daniel unto the king, I will worship the Lord my God: for he is the living God.*
>
> *But give me leave, O king, and I shall slay this dragon without sword or staff…*[30]

---

29. *Apocrypha*, "Bel and the Dragon." Chapter 1:3–22. We shall refrain from comment on how a ruler bearing the epithet "The Great" did not know his priests and their families were consuming the daily temple offerings, nor how bad it is for one's health to make a fool of a king.

30. Ibid., 23–26.

With tone-deafness that would do Washington politicians proud, Cyrus said, "Great idea! Go right ahead, kill the people's Dragon." And when Daniel did just that, the people were righteously outraged, rising up against their monarch and demanding justice. In true kingly fashion, Cyrus refused to take any responsibility for the Dragon's death, instead promptly tossing his former friend to the lions. The outcome of this tale is part of most every Sunday-school syllabus, notable here only because the lions fared far better than the Dragon—or the Dragon's followers, who became lion kibble in Daniel's stead.

Greece and Rome

In the centuries that followed the rise of monotheism, the European enchantments were hard-pressed to keep ahead of the shifting religious tide. Many from the Fertile Crescent flew west to an enclave that stretched from the eastern Mediterranean through Greece and the Balkans to the western coast of the Italian Peninsula. They established alliances with the local weyrs and peoples, being particular favorites of Pan (god of forest, field, and all things wild) and his satyrical kindred—and vice versa. This was a natural association: Pan and Dragons shared a mutual love of music, dance, and wild parties, and—like the Celts and Druids in the North—shared stewardship of sacred grottos, springs, and wooded glades. Like Dragons, Pan demanded little and gave much in return. Tales of human sacrifice are just that: tales. Dragons and gods have always been more than capable of meeting their own needs without having to shake down the populace. And together they worked wonders. During the Battle of Marathon (490 BCE), for example, with a roar that could have only been Dragon-enhanced, Pan set the invading Persians to flight and saved the Athenian forces. Revenge on those who'd driven the Dragons from their former weyrlands was, no doubt, a sweet little bonus.

Dragons also found refuge in the Pindus Mountains of northern Greece where, back in the days of their Cosmic ancestors, Apollo established the first recorded Dragon sanctuary. After overpowering the prophetic Python at Delphi, the god removed her clutch of eggs to the Pindus. There, in a golden-fenced garden, they were placed under the watchful eyes of the Dragon Epirotes. She raised them with care, ensuring Python's far-sighted line continued through the centuries. Extra Dragons would have been more than welcome, if only to occasionally relieve Epirotes from her fostering duties.

Though Dragons were a familiar part of the ancient Greek landscape, among the pre-Socratic thinkers of the time (c. 600–450 BCE) the spiritual take on them was more symbolic than literal. As Athena embodied wisdom and justice and Apollo represented reason and harmony, so Dragons were the personification of raw power and fierce loyalty. Æneas, survivor of the Trojan War and legendary wanderer, took this sense of Dragons with him when he sailed west to the Italian Peninsula, sharing it with those darn Etruscans, forefathers of the Roman people.

As Rome grew into a regional super power, Dragons unfortunately took on a more martial aspect. By the second century CE, the *draco* flew above the legions, emblematic of the empire's military might and inspiring the forces with courage. Like many things regarded today as quintessentially Roman, the history of the draco is one of assimilation, riding out of Eastern Europe with the Dacian cavalry. Dacia was a kingdom tucked between the Danube River and the Carpathian Mountains in what is today Romania and Moldova. The draco was a simple windsock used by archers to gauge wind speed and direction. Originally, it sported the head of a wolf—the sacred animal of the Dacian people. When the kingdom was absorbed by Rome (c. 106 CE), the cohorts of Emperor Marcus Aurelius took the standard, swapped the wolf for a more fiercesome Dragon, and *voilà*! It's doubtful these figures struck fear into their enemies' hearts. Thanks to the labors of Druids and Celts and Dragons cavorting among the common folk, peoples in the crosshairs of Roman expansion were on excellent footing with their local enchantments. When you know Dragons personally, you'd hardly quiver in your sandals at a windsock bearing one's image. It also helped that for many years the Roman Empire had a relatively live-and-let-live attitude towards the religious beliefs of others. As long as tributes were paid, you could worship in grove or temple, one god or many—even Dragons, if that was your inclination. Sadly, all good things come to an end.

Christianity

As BCE gave way to CE, there was a new faith on the block, and no one in draconic circles was prepared for the violence it would bring to their lives. Over the course of a couple of centuries—barely a half-life in Dragon years— Christianity exchanged cult status for that of a serious cultural force, altering the European enchantments and their alliances forever.

Judaic traditions and the anti-Dragon sentiments found in the *Tanakh* (Hebrew canon) were clearly evident in the underpinnings of this emerging belief system. It was to be expected: Satan and his minions had been running amok throughout the Holy Land—from Dan to Beersheba—for hundreds of years. But the fledgling Christians, with their evangelical zeal, took these views to a whole new level. Beginning around 180 CE when the followers of St. Paul and the traditional Roman branch of the faith splintered off from the more philosophical Gnostic branch, Dragons and Pan could kiss their revered status good-bye. The demigod with cloven hooves and goatish horns—not to mention his less than sober ways—was the archetype for the new and improved Satan. In a case of guilt by association, Dragons— horned and fiery—were as fiendish as they came. St. John was particularly adamant about their increasingly profane place in the scheme of things:

> *And there was war in heaven: Michael and his angels fought against the dragon; and the dragon fought and his angels, and prevailed not… And the great dragon was cast out, that old serpent, called the Devil…*[31]

More tolerant dracophiles are quick to point out that given John's history, a degree of paranoia about devils and Dragons is to be expected. Anyone, no matter how holy, who has survived being plunged into boiling oil and banished to a rocky patch in the Aegean is not only likely to have visions, but also see demons where there are none. While this is a generous interpretation of his anti-Dragon dogma, John, who'd surely crossed paths with Dragons both True and

---

31. King James Bible, The Revelation of St. John: 12–13; 17.

pseudo in his travels and who had experienced the pain of persecution firsthand, should have known better.

When the Emperor Constantine converted to Christianity in 312 CE, life for European Dragons went from bad to worse. Years of Judeo-Christian oppression were replaced by vengeful anti-Pagan campaigns: in an increasingly black-and-white world, conversion or death fast became the only acceptable results of Roman conquest. From one end of the empire to the other, Dragons exemplified all things Pagan and demonic—in short, all that the newly Christianized Romans found threatening and offensive. It was a new age. The wilderness was to be controlled, not revered; the sacred oaks were felled, the holy waters dammed, and their deities banished. That many sacred tribal sites and weyrs sat on prime real estate was an added incentive not to be overlooked. Dragon or Druid or would-be saint, the planet's energy grid thrums for all. It's what comes after that signifies.

Even the least educated Celts and Druids were adept at talking to Dragons. That was hardly true of the newly evangelical Romans, which made conversation out of the question, let alone conversion. Extermination became the order of the day, and there was no lack of willing participants. From the early second century CE well into the Middle Ages, aside from martyrdom—and sometimes in conjunction with it—the surest route to sainthood ran right through Dragons. Dangling the prospect of riches like a carrot before the populous, rumors of treasure hoardes for the plundering spilled forth from pulpit and palace. With fame, fortune, and papal blessings to be had, youths were lining up around the plaza.

St. George of Cappadocia (c. 275–303 CE) was the most infamous of this new breed of dragon slayer. Providing a template for his successors, he proved a persistent thorn in scaly sides long after his death. (Contrary to pro-Dragon gossip, he was not burnt to a crisp by Dragonfire but was beheaded by Emperor Diocletian for refusing to worship the right gods.) From Palestine to Britain, everyone wanted a piece of George's legend, making him a man whose truth is tangled in a knot of Sunday-school fantasy. Far from taking on one of the great Celtic Dragons, as is suggested in the tale of Dragon Hill (a rise in Oxfordshire supposedly burned bare by Dragon's blood), accepted Church doctrine put George a world away in the Holy Land near the town of Lydda on the Plain of Sharon. In such an arid spot, competition for water was fierce; to that end, a truculent desert Dragon nested protectively near the local spring. The townspeople appeased this Dragon with offerings of sheep and goats, and when that so longer sufficed, they offered maidens. Naturally, when it came time for the king's daughter to step up, an extraordinary hero was expected to ride onto the scene and turn disaster into celebration. In Lydda, George was that hero: a Roman officer from a long line of Roman officers, a Christian from a family of Christians. Under the sign of the cross, he slew the beast, saved the princess, and won the everlasting gratitude of the king and his people. Wholesale rejection of their Pagan ways naturally ensued. Latter-day skeptics insist it was a mere crocodile, not a Dragon, but crocs are not nearly as impressive and don't carry the same religious clout.

This was the beginning of a boom time for the Church and a dark, dark time for Dragons. From one end of the

Judeo-Christian (and, in time, Islamic) world to the other, Dragons were being systematically ripped from the tapestry of creation. Saints Margaret of Antioch, Samson, Clement of Metz, Florent, Ali of Samarqand—they cut a scale-littered swath across the land. Martyrs to their inherent natures, Dragons were executed so that Christianity could claim that faith conquers even the greatest monsters. (Curiously, despite the assault on True Dragons and the larger pseudo species, household dragons enjoyed increasing popularity among the masses, a testament to the link between Dragons and humans that kept the weyr fires burning even in the bloodiest of times.)

It should be noted, as bad as things were, not all persecuted Dragons fell to sword and lance: for some saints it was enough to have a draconic encounter and live to tell the tale. Or, better yet, to subdue a Dragon with kindly Christian words like Saints Petroc and Carantoc, two wise sixth-century Welsh monks who were able to produce converts *and* maintain peace with the local weyrs. Their approach, while unusual, was indicative of the affection between *Cymry* and *Ddraigs*—Welsh people and Dragons—dating back to prehistoric times.

Regardless of their methods, churchmen and churchwomen had the enchantments on the run. In the late fourth and early fifth centuries, Dragons flew deep into Celtic lands, creating a draconic explosion from France's Breton coast to Britain and adjacent isles. Like speaking to like, they found sanctuary among those who adhered to the ways of wood and water. But the new religion remained fast on their heels, using any Pagan/Dragon connection against both to lethal effect. Druids and Celts soon had too many problems of their own to offer the refugees continued support.

Philosopher Jiddu Krishnamurti (1895–1986) noted, "When one loses the deep intimate relationship with nature, then temples, mosques and churches become important."[32] This was at the heart of the medieval European mindset. Over the next six hundred years, churches, cathedrals, and monasteries were erected, and the Christian builders were not content with a little shared land, as the Druids had been. They demanded hectare upon hectare—enough for civil as well as sacred authorities, for cathedrals, castles, and towns. Our fiery friends were pushed to small pockets of virtual wasteland. Yet even *this* was not enough for some humans. The negative perceptions of Dragons were so embedded in the European hearts and minds that with the end of the first millennium approaching and end-of-days talk flitting around, an all-out interspecies war seemed inevitable.

Fortunately Dragons have a better sense of self-preservation than most people.

An assortment of adventurous young Dragons chose distance as the better part of valor and departed for the New World. Those who remained soon discovered the only allies they could count on were those who lived on the verges of the physical world, particularly the *Sidhe*, or Faërie. With their ethereal aid, by the time William I crossed the English Chanel in 1066, Queens, Sires, and Dragonlets were dancing in and out of the Otherworld waiting for the anti-Dragon lunacy to abate. (Unfortunately, in their

---

32. Krishnamurti, *Beginnings of Learning*, 236.

absence, the continent's pseudo-dragons were left to bear the brunt of human hostility. See chapter 7.) They had a long wait; the next few centuries were filled with wizards and alchemists and their mercenary Dragon hunters.

Thanks to the Romantics and their fascination with Druidry, the late eighteenth century saw Paganism creep back into European—notably British—culture. In opposition to the flow of the times, these Neo-Druids turned their backs on the Earth-fouling Industrial Age and embraced a world in which nature was celebrated, even revered. This was the opening the enchantments needed. Bit by bit, with the aid of a growing company of tree-hugging Neopagans, they came roaring back.

It is now the twenty-first century and, despite the Crusades, a Reformation, and even Vatican II, the official Church line on Dragons remains essentially unchanged. Fortunately, people are more adaptable than institutions. Since the Enlightenment (c. 1650–1800), Europeans in particular have tempered their faith with practical experience, allowing first-hand knowledge to trump dogma. Kudos! And kudos again!

Sadly, the return of religious fundamentalism and end-of-the-world zealotry has New World and Middle Eastern Dragons once more in the crosshairs of persecution. This makes them understandably jittery and defensive: a prospective crop of latter-day Georges assaulting them from helicopters and fighter jets with their high-tech weaponry is enough to send whole weyrs into hiding. Fortunately, the World Association for Dragons Everywhere (WAFDE) is joining forces with more mainstream wildlife groups in the fight against intolerance and for Dragon conservation. This is a matter of natural balance, not moral/theological relativism.

That said, as a rational species, we'd do well to remember that devils and demons are human constructs. We've fashioned them from the shadowy chaos that disturbs our sleep. We've imbued them with darkness and called them monsters. Willing to see evil in others, in those we can take arms against and slay, we forget the fiercest ethical battles are waged within, not without. Dragons have not deserved such ill treatment. Wing bumping elbow, since the beginning of time they've done nothing but be Dragons, a slice of creation no less perfect than any other. That we have distanced ourselves from their perfection is our failing, not theirs.

The Greek poet Agathon (c. 448–400 BCE) said, "This only is denied to God: the power to undo the past" (so claims Aristotle in his *Nicomachean Ethics*). True or not, a just and benevolent God should want to undo the past evil done to Dragons in his name.

seven

Dragons in Magic and Alchemy

The Cosmic Jester has long juggled religion, sorcery, and science, watching their paths cross, separate, and cross again with nimble expertise. In the process, some lines were permanently blurred and others became increasingly distinct. For enchantments, everything came together in what we've broadly termed the "occult." And with good reason: despite their understandable ambivalence and even hostility towards religion, Dragons have always managed an enthusiasm for magic. Honoring uniqueness and strength, magic never demanded conversion, never asked our friends to be any less than 100 percent Dragon, 100 percent of the time. Of course, nothing else would do: watering down Dragon natures diminishes the power of Dragon wizardry to the point where a mage might as well be working with a gecko.

From talismans and spellcasting to the mysteries of the stars, from medicine and metallurgy to the intricacies of alchemical formulae, the respect with which we wove Dragon power into our arcane arts tickled them silly. (That is, of course, until the weaving became literal and Dragons found themselves as little more than ingredient providers for alchemists and their minions.) Peasant or mage (or as was often the case, peasant/mage), for those who could see Dragons' power, they were a beacon lighting the way between ancient and modern worlds. Dragons danced along the cutting edge, just waiting for us to follow.

Like many things of cultural and draconic significance, this Dragon two-step was thought to have originated in the East. Given that Europe was groping about in the Dark Ages (c. 400–900 CE) while China and Japan were flourishing, this is a logical assumption. The spiritual groundwork laid by Laozi and Confucius, combined with appreciations of arts, sciences, philosophy, and politics, created richly layered societies. To many a crypto-anthropologist, the benevolent give and take between enchantments and humans made the East's global standing a virtual no-brainer.

Though venerating the East over the West in terms of Dragon treatment is a neat way of looking at things, it's not entirely accurate. The empirical wonders of Egypt, Greece, Persia, and Rome were each extraordinary and, as we have seen, Dragon inspired. To weigh Egypt's Great Pyramids and Babylon's Hanging Gardens against the accomplishments of the Zhou Dynasty is like comparing snallygasters and lindworms—apples and orangutans. With a draconic presence from the international date line to the prime meridian, real historical differences came not in the long-long-ago, but in the middle of the first millennium CE. These were years of great intellectual and cultural growth, the threshold of the coming alchemical revolution that tempered superstition with science and placed Dragons at the core of scholastic discourse.

Sympathetic Magic

But none of this would have been possible without the groundwork of sympathetic magic. First discussed by Sir James George Frazer (1854–1941) in his classic study, *The Golden Bough*, sympathetic magic is one of the oldest forms of the art. Simply put, it is based on the assumption that a person (or thing) can be affected by use of their name or an object representing them—by the practitioner being "in sympathy" with their subject.[33] This is the premise behind everything from charms and cave paintings to icons and prayers. Dragons and sympathetic magic go back to a time of nature-based faiths that bound Dragon and human together. To a time when the strange and unexplained were the province of sorcerers.

Sorcerers were considered remnants from the older shamanic traditions. They kept to the wilderness, villages at most, offering their services as mediators with the natural—i.e., draconic—world when needed. These magic practitioners were necessary but suspect, their abilities making them both awe-inspiring and vulnerable. Their similarities and connections with the great Dragons were not only noticed

---

33. See *Golden Bough*, 11–48.

but useful. Not that Dragons made good familiars; anything but. They're far too wild and independent for such a symbiotic relationship even with a powerful, compassionate mage. At best, they were allies.

This alliance was defined by the sorcerers' elemental connection with Dragons, one in which water, earth, wood, fire, and (in the East) metal, were manipulated and celebrated. Your average villager likely viewed this interaction as holy, which is understandable in a world where sorcerer-priests were not uncommon. Yet what passed for sacred magic was essentially a matter of linguistics: sorcerers could speak Dragonese. Fabulous but not necessarily paranormal, these clever individuals were simply using the knowledge and resources (Dragons) at hand to solve the problems of their day. This was particularly evident in the Orient. When the winds stilled and the fields cracked with drought, a sorcerer would speak to the local Dragon King (or Queen—there is no gender bias among Dragons), imploring him to use his command of air and water to refresh the land. When winter lay long and heavy upon the land, Lung Wang, the Fire Dragon, would be invoked to melt the snows and warm the soil.

Of course, just being able to communicate with a Dragon is no guarantee that one's requests will be well received. Dragons, like gods, can always say no. To hedge against this possibility, the people turned to amulets, carvings, festivals, and other forms of everyday sympathetic magic. Such populist practices were of particular interest to the Dragons, appealing to their more democratic instincts. Royalty and wizards are too used to having others do their bidding, an attitude that does not go over well around the weyrs. Demanding anything of their kind is considered by Dragons the height of arrogance, especially coming from such crushable creatures with tin hats and inflated egos.

What about the sorceress Medea and Yu the Great, you ask, who had Dragons in harness, pulling their chariots across the heavens? As most Dragons will remind you, these were (1) myths, and (2) instances of *deus ex machina*—God from a machine. The Dragons were working at divine behest, not mortal. In the case of Medea—princess, priestess of Hecate (Greek goddess of magic), and sorceress *extraordinaire*—this was not as simple as it might appear. Her reputation among the local enchantments had suffered considerably as a result of her drugging the Dragon of Colchis so that Jason could steal the Golden Fleece. Years later, when Jason threw Medea over for a new princess, the sun god Helios sent a Dragon-drawn chariot to spirit her away from Corinth and the fallout of her homicidal vengeance (though given what we know of Dragons today, it was far more likely she rode astride a lone Dragon to safety). Helios was Medea's grandfather, and he carried considerable weight with the weyrs of ancient Greece. Yet, had the sorceress allowed Jason to slay the Dragon as her father had tasked him to, appeals from Zeus himself could not have moved them to raise a wingtip in her aid. As it turned out, the draconic proportions of Medea's retribution likely inspired them to overlook that little incident with the drugs. Medea may have been unlucky in love, but she was very lucky with Dragons.

When dealing with Dragons, remember: king or commoner, never demand, never expect, and never, ever ask them to wear a harness.

In the realm of everyday magic, the wide-eyed appreciation of the people certainly moved Dragons more than regal commands. In a simple charm or soaring kite, backed by fervent belief, Dragons found more respect, more acknowledgment of their nature, than in all the embroidered silks in the Forbidden City. For routine purposes, the people did not need go-betweens; they knew Dragons were beings so powerful that the mere image of them was a whisker away from supernatural intervention.

And how varied those images were! From metal charms stamped with "Dragon" in *kanji* (calligraphic characters) to elaborately carved shrine guardians and *netsuke* (miniature sculptures used to toggle kimono pouches closed), each picture served to link humans with the particular Dragons in their ken. In China, for example, the nine types of Dragon each had their own way of being portrayed for maximum effect. These representations were on a par with what we would today consider "public art." Mage, monk, and miller all knew the specific Dragon energy being appealed to based on the style and location of the draconic image.

The first Dragon with his thunderous voice is cast in bells and gongs that they might sound loud and clear. The second is carved into fiddles—the two-stringed *erhu*, the twenty-five-stringed *se*, and everything in between—because Dragons love music and will bless both the instrument and the player. The third is etched into stone writing tablets in recognition of Dragons' fondness of all things literary and, for some, the belief that the Cosmic Dragon Kan Je gave writing to humanity (hence the word *kanji* for written script). Everyone knows Dragons can support great weights, so around the base of stone monuments is carved the image of the fourth Dragon. Temple eaves are adorned with the fifth, as Dragons are always wide-eyed against danger. Dragons being creatures of water, the sixth can be found on bridge timbers, to ensure strength against floods and roiling tides. The seventh Dragon blesses the Buddha's throne, acknowledging the affection between enchantments and the Enlightened One and their mutual fondness for a good rest.

The last two Dragon images draw on dark energy, the sort that rumbles through the mysterious side of nature and is found in all large, wild, powerful creatures, no matter how intelligent or sweet and cuddly they may appear. Warriors call upon the eighth Dragon, inscribing him on the hilts of their swords. They know he can be violent and unleash unspeakable slaughter and that his image will make them invincible on the battlefield—that and a good suit of paper armor styled after dense Dragon plating. The ninth has a less favorable placement; carved into prison gates, he is there as a symbol of the Dragon's fondness for causing trouble and breaking the rules. He is also a reminder that all of us—even those outside the law—are children of the Dragon.

Charms and amulets are a more personal sort of magic, not only calling on the Dragon without, but also tapping the Dragon within. Realistic representations or simple abstracts, some little more than vaguely draconic forms, when placed against one's skin they release all the strength, wisdom, creativity, luck, and sheer lust for life of the originals. They're literally portals to the Dragon we all carry within us.

The material from which these images were made was also significant, with jade and ironwood being most popular. Jade tapped into the watery side of Dragons; ironwood, their strength. And then there were those purported to be made from actual Dragon parts. Unscrupulous charm vendors were known to pass off crudely shaped flints as Dragon scales and whale teeth as Dragon fangs, a practice which could get them into grave trouble with both enchantments and civil authorities. The rank stupidity of the deceit was particularly evident in rural regions, where Dragons were part of the everyday experience and even a child could tell a Dragon scale from a chipped piece of stone.

In keeping with the cultural attitudes of the West, European Dragons were largely invoked for their ferocity and bravado. This was especially true following the decline of the Druids, and it did little to alter the increasingly grim perception of Dragons in the Dark Ages. (The enchantments no doubt lamented this representation, preferring less warfare in their names and more cliff-diving off Denmark's Faroe Isles.) In tattoos and pendants, heroes and kings claimed Dragons as their personal guardians. The Dragon-headed longships of Scandinavia, for example, honored those who ruled the sea, imploring their favor for fair winds and fierce fighting at journey's end. Though less refined than their Eastern counterparts, the warrior chieftains of the region claimed the magic of their local Dragons and kept it alive. Of course, Dragons are far more democratic than royalty wish to acknowledge. As in China and Japan, fisher folk from the Mediterranean to the North Atlantic pocketed simple Dragon charms for protection and an abundant catch. Inland peoples looked to inland Dragons—True and pseudo—fingering their talismans as they beseeched diggers and drakes to lead them to deposits of iron, copper, and gold. Such actions mirror those of early Chinese prospectors who never left home without their charms honoring Fu-Ts'ang, the Dragon of Hidden Treasures.

Dragons and Astrology

Much as Dragons appreciated their likenesses slicing through the waves and twining up the scrawny arms of bewhiskered Vikings, in time such simple sorcery was not enough for them. They were greater than that, and if humans didn't see it on their own, then they would have to be shown. Dragons were about to take their place among the stars.

This brings us to the rise of astrology and the attendant shift towards a more metaphysical and physical (alchemical) view of Dragons and their influence. Indeed, some consider astrology the first step we took out of the shadows of superstition, into the dawning light of scientific enlightenment.

In the East, the high standing Dragons enjoyed placed them not only in the heavens, like the Greek Draco, but as a key player in the Oriental zodiac. Of course, some dracophiles insist that Draco, wending his way across the sky from Ursa Major to Ursa Minor, is as influential as the stellar *lung*—if not more so—for Draco touches not one but all houses of the Western zodiac.

Despite Dragons being equal-opportunity benefactors, it's believed those born in their Chinese zodiacal year are most attuned to the creatures and are thus due the greatest measure of their protection. Chinese astrologers went on to break their impact down further. They held that, while all human "Dragons" are driven, confident, and (essentially) honest, the subtleties of their personalities are influenced by the guiding element of their particular birth year: wood, fire, earth, metal, or water. *Note that the Chinese year begins and ends in late January or early February, depending on the exact year. The Gregorian years listed are when the Chinese year begins.*

Wood Dragons are creative and curious, capable of bold, out-of-the-box thinking. Less egocentric than others of their kind, they are logical, pragmatic, even willing to compromise when needs be. Do not be fooled by this get-along aspect: they will speak their mind and fight courageously if challenged. Wood Dragons years include 1904, 1964, and 2024.

As one might imagine, Fire Dragons are the most volatile of the quintet. They are also charismatic and extremely competitive, giving nothing short of their best. And this is what they expect from friends and coworkers, inspiring them by example and personal magnetism. On the flip side, their sense of their own superiority—merited or not—leads them to be short on the humility scale. If things don't go their way, they can get downright snappish. But, if mindful of their shortcomings, there is nothing they cannot achieve. Fire Dragon years include 1916 and 1976.

Earth Dragons are, well, down-to-earth. They are steady and thoughtful, facing challenges with almost diplomatic aplomb. They appreciate other points of view, even if they don't share them, an approach that makes them less tyrannical and more even-tempered than other Dragons. Consequently, any Earth Dragon who loses his temper has been pushed very hard, indeed. Earth Dragon years include 1928 and 1988.

If you know what's good for you, never cross a Metal Dragon. True to their element, they are rigid and aggressive, lacking in empathy to the point of being cruelly oblivious to others. They will rise to the top because it's all they know how to do; should work, social, even family relationships be trashed along the way, that is simply the price of Metal Dragon ambition. Metal Dragon years include 1940 and 2000.

Finally, there are Water Dragons. The least selfish of the lot, they are flexible, able to give and take, to compromise— even accept defeat graciously—where others would just dig in their heels and roar. They will even surrender power if it contributes to the greater good. Water Dragons are excellent negotiators, knowing just when to push and when to ease off. If they have a failing, it is excessive optimism, which sometimes blinds them to a no-win situation. That said, the Water Dragon's laid-back nature—at times verging on shy—makes them easy to be around. They are draconic delights. Water Dragon years include 1952 and 2012.

Though being born at any time has its ups and downs, the Year of the Dragon has always been considered extremely lucky, so much so that people have been known to plan their families around the Dragon's appearance every twelve years. Some imperial astrologers, fearing for their lives, were even suspected of fudging dynastic birthdates so their emperors might believe themselves blessed by the Dragon's favor. Not that one can blame them: in the days of war lords and dynastic upheavals, it was every prince for himself and every advantage—perceived or real—helped.

For all its scientific trappings, astrology is, at heart, still a form of sympathetic magic. The weight it carries lies in the honor and affection with which Dragons are held. Beyond that, belief works wonders.

Dragons and Alchemy

Decade after decade, civilization as we know it inched away from magical thinking and towards a more objective, empirical, scientific view of the world. This was the complex field of alchemy in which chemistry, medicine, and physics were all wrapped up with a dollop of the mystical in an effort to transform the ordinary into the extraordinary. As an emerging discipline, alchemy was ripe to spread across the world on the backs of Dragons.

Where magic—especially in its simplest, no-need-to-be-gods form—was open to all, alchemists came almost exclusively from scholarly (some might say orthodox) religious environments. This came as no surprise in the Orient, where Taoism and Buddhism had been combining philosophy, mysticism, and naturalistic studies for generations. By the first century CE, monasteries in China and Japan were *the* centers of learning. There, in a mix of academics and faith, great strides were made in the physical, formal, and natural sciences. Gunpowder, high-tensile steel, and a veritable pharmacopeia were the products of monastic scholarship and experimentation.

In Europe, the heyday of the alchemists came later, starting around 1100 CE. Outside the occasional abbey wall, the Dark Ages were marked by a deplorable lack of classical learning. Combine that lack with the Church's deep suspicion of all things beyond the official Creed (including Dragons), and it was a wonder Europe didn't lose her civilization entirely. Thanks to Druids, Moors from North Africa, and a few Irish monks, pockets of learning remained. These, in time, gave birth to medieval Scholasticism (c. 1100 CE), out of which came a new academic environment in which alchemists could thrive.

Across the globe, the Philosopher's Stone was the alchemists' obsession. That said, seekers split into two camps—East and West—regarding the purposes to which this legendary substance would be put. In the East, the Stone was valued primarily as aid in creating the Elixir of Eternal Life. Though the Elixir itself was never found, extraordinary medicinal breakthroughs were made as a result of the effort. In the West, a more materialistic attitude sought the Philosopher's Stone as the means to change base metals into gold. This is a generalized perspective, of course; there were crossovers in both traditions: fourteenth-century French alchemist Nicolas Flamel's quest for eternal life is legend (and not just in Harry Potter books), as are the metallurgical works of the great Oriental swordsmiths.

One way or another, as both inspiration and source materials, Dragons had a paw in just about all of it. In fact, some believed they fit the new world almost too well. No other creature embodies the combination of physical and metaphysical, symbolic and literal, the way Dragons do. It was little wonder the early alchemists considered Dragon observation the best teaching tool imaginable. As mentioned before, Dragons are essentially equal-opportunity elementals. Yet for those who studied them, their intimate association with fire was of the greatest interest. True, water wears mountains into sand and turns barren plains green, and winds carry seeds and clouds across the heavens. But fire, dangerous and transformative to its core, excites the air with magic. It's the archetypal alchemical element, able to change the essential nature of things with a lick, to turn iron into steel and sand into glass. And no creatures—not even humans—understood flames as well as Dragons.

From the Dragon's mastery of fire, artisans learned the basics of smithing, how to make soft copper into strong bronze, refine iron into steel, and cast bells that ring true. Through the ages, advancements in metallurgy were the natural offshoots of this wisdom long-shared with craftsman and sage. Valued though these skills were, alchemical minds turned to more esoteric, less practical activities, like how Dragon breath extracted quicksilver from the ore cinnabar until it flowed in mercurial rivers. Mercury, they believed, was the First Matter out of which all other metals were formed. It was the link between the physical and the metaphysical, the key to transmutation and the Philosopher's Stone.

Medicines and the Elixir of Life

Under Taoist influences, the Eastern alchemists were less concerned with amassing material wealth than with the pursuit of scientific and medicinal discoveries. It was believed that the purification of body and spirit—the ultimate balancing of yin and yang—would lead to immortality. To this end, traditional cures such as herbs, honey, even wine, were combined with more hazardous elements—mercury, lead, arsenic—resulting in treatments at times beneficial but often extremely dangerous. Notably harmed by these endeavors was Chinese king/emperor Qin Shi Huang (259–210 BCE) of terracotta-army fame. So determined was he to achieve immortality that he tried an array of "elixirs," including one made of mercury and powdered jade, which only hastened his death. On a more productive hand, the use of arsenic to treat syphilis, internal parasites, and certain cancers can be traced to these early alchemical experiments.

Unfortunately, for the first time in local weyr memory, this quest for health and long life resulted in a misunderstanding that placed Dragons in a perilous position. According to lore and the reasoning of the age, nothing was more beneficial than a remedy concocted with herbs, metallic compounds, and pieces of Dragon.

How, in a culture steeped in reverence for these wondrous beings, did people start using Dragon bits and pieces for their own gain? As with many things Dragon, the problem arose out of ignorance and the wrongs resulting from it. First, let's remember that Dragons were viewed as change incarnate. Year after year, from newborn Dragonlet to hoary Elder, they sloughed their skin, shedding the old for the new, becoming constantly more than they once were. Proper alchemists knew the ultimate strength of the Dragon lay in her mature totality. To separate her into parts weakens her beyond imagining, not to mention being extremely bad form. That said, they were familiar enough with the species to know that what is left behind through the natural process of growth and transformation retains some measure of the creature's power. Molted Dragon skins, for example, were reported to be so full of yang energy that they glowed like the sun.[34] The potency of such a find could not be denied by scholar or fool.

It was in this environment that, long ago, some local healer with a curious mind and a passing acquaintance

---

34. Visser, *Dragon in China and Japan,* 94.

with Dragons chanced upon a shed scale one day, ground it up, mixed it in his tea, and felt twenty years younger. It wouldn't have been a True Dragon scale—they are too hard to grind by ancient means; it was probably from a kiau (marsh dragon) or some lowland digger. Still, thanks to the high concentration of vitamins and minerals not normally found in the human diet, its healthful effects would likely have felt magical. And so the first step on a slippery slope was taken. If a scale was good, perhaps a claw or horn was better. Bones, hair, teeth, skin, internal organs, fetuses, blood...? The list of possible wonder cures was endless, as was that of ailments in need of them. One thing led to another until there was a new and dubious discipline branching off from mainstream alchemical science: Dragon medicine. Its practitioners, with questionable science but often the best of intentions, were soon serving up potions for everything from dysentery to paralysis.[35] It should be noted that Dragon medicine is, in a way, the ultimate in sympathetic magic: by ingesting part of the Dragon you not only get the curative properties of the medicine but become intricately caught up in a game of Six Degrees of Dragon Separation. You literally become part Dragon.

In no time at all, this new field illustrated the growing split between empirical Dragon scholarship and subjective Dragon lore, resulting in a conflicting collection of impossibilities, not least of which was the purported draconic slicing and dicing. Despite the cultural respect for the species, Dragon vivisectionists insisted they could strip a crea-

---

35. Ibid., 90–96.

ture to the bone for the greater good—and use the bones as well—in the name of eternal life, virility, wisdom, and other draconic virtues.

Neither Dragons nor the people who knew them intimately would allow such abuse. Well equipped in their own defense, True Dragons also sport blood so corrosive it eats through everything it touches—including the remains of the fallen and any potential profits. (This is one of the true things about that legend of St. George and Dragon Hill. See chapter 6.) On the human side of things, the weyrs of China and Japan were subject to Imperial sanctions severe enough to deter all but the most desperate or well-connected of poachers. Unfortunately, pseudo and mundane species were far more vulnerable under both natural and dynastic law, and the prospect of turning a blind eye and a quick *yen* often put them in the slayer's crosshairs. An environment of deception and outright false advertising was created in the marketplace. Hunters swore to buyers that their booty was genuine Dragon; when cornered by the constabulary, these same folks insisted that they only peddled lowly pseudo-dragon bits or, more likely, turtle shells and narwhal tusks (also popularly palmed off as unicorn horns).

While all this trickery may have spared a poacher or two from the executioner's blade, its effect on the evolution of the healing arts is much harder to assess. Legend and scholarship alleged that only the parts of True Dragons produced results, yet it is possible the public's gullibility and desire to partake in the power of the Dragon—in conjunction with a course of herbs and acupuncture—did indeed work what then passed for medical wonders.

Even serious alchemists who had studied Dragons up close and personal for years would gladly use the occasional dash of Dragon should it cross their path. They would be foolish not to. But those in the know knew that what is cast off is much different from what is taken. Alchemists were supposed to protect the enchantments; breaking faith with them would be a direct assault on Dragons' spirits and abilities. These individuals also understood the branding power of words in a way that would turn modern admen green with envy, using the label "Dragon" with symbolic intent on a variety of mineral, vegetable, and (mundane) animal products. Dragon's blood—used to stop bleeding and treat intestinal ailments—is not the vital fluid drawn from a Sky Dragon's veins but the carmine resin of the Dracaena tree. The name was also given to the more toxic cinnabar (mercury sulfide), a standard element in the mythical Elixir of Life. Dragon's tongue is a flowering herb used to ease coughs and chest congestion and to flavor the rare bowl of soup; Dragon's tail is a creeper with powerful anti-cancer properties; and Dragon fruit is just tasty. The rarest of the "Dragon" elements were Dragon's eyes, magnetic crystals extracted from the heads of eel and koi (aka Dragon carp). In nature these stones helped their hosts navigate in accord with the planet's magnetic fields; among alchemists, they were used to balance one's *qi* (life force), open one's mystical third eye, block pain, and aid the directionally challenged.

Scholasticism, Hoarding, and the Philosopher's Stone
Prior to the Middle Ages, European alchemy was considered less science and more dark art, its practitioners coming from the noble wizarding tradition that included the

Greek philosopher Heraclitus (535–475 BCE); the legendary trio of Taliesin from Wales, Väinämöinen of Finland,
and Siglorel the Saracen; and nameless Druid, Gnostic, and
Pagan sorcerers. Like their Oriental counterparts, these
were inspired, Dragon-friendly individuals. They looked
upon the enchantments and marveled: in scaled beauty they
saw fire and water, the physical and metaphysical, at play in
the world. They observed draconic form and function and
saw mathematic perfection and prototypes for flasks, bot-
tles, and subliming pots. After all, who could not marvel at
the crick of a Dragon's tail and see the shape of a distilling
retort just waiting to get out? Modern Dragon keepers are
indebted to the ancient alchemists for the *athanor*, an elaborate furnace designed to maintain constant temperatures
over long periods of time. Though tweaked though the ages,
the athanor is clearly the ancestor of the hatching kilns used
today for incubating Dragon eggs. In short, the wizards
worked with these creatures and learned from them. And
when their mysterious world fell under Church authority
and drove Dragons and wizards underground, they were
there to watch each others' backs.

The Dark Ages—the tenth and eleventh centuries CE,
known in draconic circles as the Dark Times—were aptly
named for Dragon and alchemist alike. True, they were a
turbulent time marked by barbaric invasions and the crum-
bling of the Roman Empire. But one wonders if Rome
would have fallen so completely had the newborn Church
not sought to obliterate the culture and learning of the classical Mediterranean world. In a celebration of ignorance as
a powerful repressive force, the masses remained virtually
illiterate; even the clergy and aristocracy were expected to

subsist on Scripture alone. Who needed Aristotle's take on ethics when you had St. Paul's epistles? Or the questions raised by Plato's *Republic* when the Kingdom of God was at hand? With the Vulgate Bible commissioned by Pope Damasus I in 382 CE, the New Testament was culled and ordered. The formal canon continued to evolve, yet, by the fifth century, the ruling powers made it very clear that anyone with knowledge (*gnosis*) of classical or occult science—not to mention their draconic cohorts—were heretics and should be hounded and hunted as unholy agents of Satan. While alchemy was always viewed as an elite study full of closely guarded secrets, secrecy was literally a matter of life and death from the fourth to the eleventh centuries.

Oddly, it was the Crusades—violently fundamentalist and Dragon-free though they were—that helped break through the short-sighted provincialism strangling Western civilization. Crusaders returning from the Holy Land brought with them not only gold and gems, but also intellectual treasures gleaned from philosophers and alchemists in Byzantium and the Middle East. Such a bounty of knowledge was inspirational to those churchmen-turned-scholars who were about to haul Europe out of the darkness and into the coming light of the Renaissance.

At the dawn of the new millennium, a window of enlightenment seemed to open in the personage of Pope Sylvester II (c. 946–1003), a man who, as a young priest in Spain, had studied the science and mathematics of the Moors. Though his enemies accused him of being in league with the devil, Sylvester is more accurately remembered as a beacon of learning in a backward time. His influence led to the subsequent rise of Scholasticism, with its melding of theology and physical and metaphysical studies (including a resurrection of classical Greek philosophy—Aristotelian and Neo-Platonist). In turn, this new and approved academic environment lent a fleeting air of respectability to alchemy. Naturally, it did not apply retroactively to wizards, Pagans, or Dragons, but a handful of preeminent theologians of the thirteenth century—such as Albertus Magnus and Roger Bacon—were granted Papal dispensations to explore the "dark arts." The trouble was, they were still clerics—high-ranking clerics—and, as such, were restricted by Church doctrine in all its anti-Dragon glory. These men may have dabbled in the occult, yet they were so far from their wizarding predecessors that most viewed Dragons as mere bestiary parables fast on their way to becoming faërie tales. For even the most open-minded of these scholars, learning Dragonese was out of the question.

This was not the best of all possible worlds, but in defense of properly obscure pursuits, it should be pointed out that not all the rising stars in the scholastic firmament were Dragon illiterate. Some of the greats, particularly those from the monastic tradition of the British Isles, such as William of Ockham (1288–1348) and the monk Johannes de Sacrobosco (1195–1256), were surely acquainted with the weyrs. Even Albertus Magnus, born in Bavaria, would have known his share of Schwarzwald Stachelrücken (Black Forest Pricklebacks) as a child. That they chose to put away these youthful experiences when they took to cowl and tonsure speaks to the absolute power of medieval Christian orthodoxy.

It did not take long for the Holy See to decide that alchemical studies were just too tainted by the devil's influence to remain sanctioned, even under the strictest rules and regulations. By the early fourteenth century, religion and the arcane sciences were definitely on the outs again. This did not stop the celebrated minds of the day from pushing the knowledge envelope; it simply forced such activities back into the shadows. With the best education in medieval Europe coming from religious (though increasingly humanistic) universities, individuals pursuing answers to the strange and mystical often retained strong Church ties, many actually being bound by holy orders. It was a good cover: public clerics by day becoming closeted seekers of supernatural wisdom by night. Sadly, these individuals were hard pressed to shake the Church's intolerance for Dragons and wizards of Dragon acquaintance.

The effect this had on the continent's enchantments is impossible to calculate. The wizards were all but gone, and Dragon numbers were seriously diminished; those who hung on were fast withdrawing from humanity's spread. True Dragons would likely have kept to themselves, given the chance. Unfortunately, we did not give it to them.

Though public dialogue was increasingly dismissive of Dragons, they were making a comeback behind closed laboratory doors, their active hoarding and vital fire considered the blessed focus of an alchemist's existence. With increased attention to transmuting base metals into gold, myths of treasures dating back to those of the great Dragons Ladon and Fafnir were about to have a mash-up with quasirational thought. One of the more troublesome stories circulating around the cloisters was of the Dragon's Stone—the weyr equivalent to the elusive Philosopher's Stone—which every Dragon reportedly used to feather their nests. If only these creatures could be caught, studied, their mysterious Dragon's Stone found and analyzed! And if you have a Dragon in hand, you might as well take him apart, too, find out what makes him tick, how his organs work, what rare and unusual properties his Dragonfire possesses... In the name of inquiring minds (not to mention imagined riches and chalking up brownie points with the Pope), Dragons were fast on their way to becoming the lab rats of any alchemist who could afford them.

Though seldom going into the field to procure these creatures firsthand, well-heeled alchemists were not above employing freelance Dragon hunters to do their dirty work. Home from the wars and in need of livelihood, the countryside was rife with swordsmen for hire. These mercenaries were no match for True Dragons, however; like their Asian counterparts, the hunters went after pseudo species with relish. Fen flappers, Breton yannigs, even Iberian amphipteres—it was open season on them all. Against this gruesome onslaught, the dragons gave as good as they got, though many of the smaller, shier species were simply overwhelmed. The addition of gunpowder to the human arsenal in the thirteenth century only made the balance of power more disparate. As a matter of sheer motivation, it did not help the draconic cause that, with a little shameless post-slaying self-promotion, a threadbare ex-Crusader could dine out for years on a well-spun Dragon tale. He had only to convince the locals that he'd made their corner of the world safe (and could keep it that way)—a line that carried a lot of weight in the perilous Middle Ages. Of course, it all depended on a good sales pitch: chances are the townsfolk hadn't seen a real Dragon in years.

Back at the laboratory, though the Philosopher's Stone remained out of reach, the general consensus was that real progress was being made in the sciences. Much in the way of modern pharmacologists, medieval doctors, naturalists, and venomologists insisted on the necessity of using pseudo-dragons (as well as numerous mundane species) in their experiments. Various books of poisons were all the rage in their day, and most noted the lethal properties of such compounds as powdered tarasca horn and wyvern tears (how wyvern tears were extracted does not bear imagining!). Karma having its place in all things, many apothecaries who got their hands dirty with these substances themselves experienced agonizing ends as a result of prolonged exposure.

Modern cryptoherpetologists—indeed, all people of conscience—look upon these predatory practices with utter contempt. The methodology was shameless in terms of Dragon conservation, not to mention being severely short on scientific credibility. Draconic experiments and their suspect results were largely ignored during the Renaissance; come the eighteenth-century Enlightenment, reference to Dragons was all but lost in the brittle margins of rare books and parchments. After the fifteenth century, even illustrious scholars like Leonardo da Vinci, Paracelsus, and Isaac Newton relegated Dragons to figurative citations in bestiaries and fictions. Though instrumental in leading us to the scientific frontier, Western Dragons were quickly forgotten among the academic community. They were just too fanciful for an increasingly objective intellectual world. As it turned out, this was just the breather Dragons needed: with the heat taken off the weyrs, they were able to regroup and revive.

Today scientists and those who pursue alchemical arts are loath to slip Dragons into their equations. This reluctance is more indicative of the cynical times in which we live than an absence of scaled inspiration. In 1676, Isaac Newton, father of modern science, wrote to fellow scientist Robert Hooke, "If I have seen further it is only by standing on the shoulders of giants." He might well have added "and by dancing on the wings of Dragons." From primitive spells to unraveling the physical intricacies of our universe, we are indebted to our magical friends, great and small, now until the end of time.

Dragons in Literature and the Arts

In the ancient wilds of northern Europe, there was a warrior who became a king. With raised shield and bloody blade, this bear of a man battled mortals and monsters, losing friends and fellows yet winning fame. If he was boastful at times, even vain, it was no more than his hero's due. As is too often the way with heroes, he came to believe he was as invulnerable as the bards said. Even with his beard white and step slowed, when a Dragon roiled through the countryside avenging a theft from his lair, the king took up sword and shield and went forth to meet the foe of his old age.

He told his men the fight was not theirs,

> *... nor meet for any but me alone.*
> *To measure might with this monster here.*
> *And play the hero.*[36]

A fierce battle ensued—the Dragon was protecting his lair and life, after all—and though the king was true to his word and slew the great creature, he was himself slain in return. Thus, against the Dragon Hordshyrde, Beowulf had his last hurrah, and, with the stroke of a pen, Dragons— particularly in the West—thundered out of lore and onto the imaginary stage.

It was over a thousand years ago that an anonymous Anglo-Saxon bard put *Beowulf* on paper; with the passage of time, Dragons' place in the literary and artistic world has only become more secure. And is it any wonder? Dragons are the heart and soul of once-upon-a-time, embraced as a veritable *tabula rasa* (blank slate) upon which can be laid any creative notion or pop-psychology trend of the day. In short, Dragons could be whatever your story needed them to be. These were creatures of the imagination, beyond the bounds of fact or faith. It should be noted that, for centuries, this was a largely Western phenomenon: the reality and religion of Dragons so vital to the East essentially kept Asian Dragons in the oral tradition but out of literature. They are only just beginning to make their presence felt in films and the like, no doubt waiting for our technical expertise to advance to where they can be represented in

---

36. *Beowulf,* Episode XXXV, lines 2541–44. It should be noted that Beowulf did not go it alone but got help/rescue from his friend Wiglaf.

all their glory. (And no, Godzilla and Rodan are not even remotely related to Dragons.)

On the other hand, European Dragons have been players in tales of high adventure and derring-do for centuries, symbolic of the villainous forces swirling through the world. In these chivalric sagas, elements of politics and romance were essential to the mix: a Dragon's demise earned you the keys to the kingdom and the hand of fair maiden for good measure. The eighteenth century saw Dragons soaring through pages of faërie tales, consorting with witches and wizards as emblems of our darkest psychological fears and the ultimate obstacles for the would-be hero in us all. Come modern times, our friends finally had a creative landscape in which they could thrive in all their complexity, at turns glorious, wild, dangerous, and wise.

Aside from the fact that the artistic world insists on lumping them into the "fantasy" genre, for contemporary Dragons, anything goes. Good or evil, wise or purely intuitive, taciturn or verbose, Dragons are no longer tied to knightly affairs, but have lives of their own. Though more fleshed out, they are still whatever and whoever the storyteller needs them to be. Not even Dragons can escape the tyranny of the writer's pen.

The paintings, poems, novels, and films featuring Dragons are too numerous for a detailed A–Z study, but over the next few pages, we will take a look at a representative cross section, spanning the centuries.

Chivalrous Tales and Renaissance Allegory

Dragons in King Arthur's Court

Mention the Age of Chivalry and the mind leaps to tales of righteous knights in burnished armor and maidens in dire need of rescue. And no tale exemplified this like *Le Morte d'Arthur*. Written in the fifteenth century by Sir Thomas Malory, this classic account of King Arthur and his knights and times was sourced from the twelfth-century works of Welsh cleric Geoffrey of Monmouth and French poet Chrétien de Troyes. Despite being a man of the Renaissance, Malory held onto the medieval qualities of these sources. He romanticized a rough-and-tumble time, instilling it with ideals of might for right, king and country (state), God (religion), and fair damsel (courtly love). Ironically, Malory was anything but chivalrous himself: a thief, a rapist, political conspirator, and all-round reprobate, he spent most of his adult life either locked up or on the lam. It is believed he wrote his masterwork while serving a stretch at the King's pleasure in Newgate Prison. Still, Arthurian gallantry was his literary backdrop, and in this landscape, a Dragon was the ultimate test of a knight's worth.

Though several Round Table companions faced this challenge, none met the test like Launcelot du Lac. In an adjunct to the tale of Sir Tristram of Lyoness (who had his own draconic encounters), Malory wrote of Launcelot's exploits at the Grail Castle, exploits which produced epic ripples throughout Arthur's realm.[37] The gist of the tale is this: following some cryptic words from a visiting hermit, Launcelot rode out from

---

37. See Malory, *Le Morte d'Arthur*, 335–58.

Camelot, as was his habit, in search of adventure. In the green hills of Wales—no strangers to Dragons—he came upon Pointe Corbyn, the Grail Castle. This was a place of magic and prophecy, home to King Pelles, his daughter, and a Dragon.

The Dragon was the fire-breathing bane of the town and the object of a grave prophecy: "He who slays the serpent will sire the purest knight the world has ever known." Never one to turn down a challenge, Launcelot did battle with the creature and prevailed in true heroic fashion. A grateful King Pelles embraced him like a long lost son—or longed-for son-in-law—and Launcelot got his first glimpse of the Holy Grail and a mystical earful about Round Table quests to come. Mindful of the words on the Dragon's "tomb" (lair), the king set about getting the hero into bed with his daughter, Elaine. Under normal circumstances, this should have been a matter of course: knight slays Dragon, knight wins the hand of the princess. Simple. But this was Launcelot, a man besotted by his not-so-courtly love for Queen Gwynevere. Still, what matters is a grand passion—or the feelings of one's daughter—when up against divine prophecy? One thing led to another and with the help of a magical potion and more than a little deceit, ol' Lance was tricked into sleeping with Elaine. The next morning, following this flagrant breach of hospitality and etiquette, a mortified Launcelot nearly took the fair lady's head off. Only her beauty and quick-witted appeal to his chivalrous nature saved her. Nine months later, Galahad was born—pure as the Cambrian snows and destined to surpass his father in all things, especially those Grail-related.

So it was that the death of one Dragon changed the course of many lives. But what did Malory intend the Dragon to represent? Briefly put, he was the enemy of the three prongs of chivalric service: God, state, and women. As one would expect from the tale's setting, the Dragon was first and foremost the personification of that old-time religion of the Druids and Celts. This was the faith of Merlin—wizard, sage, and advisor to kings—who had a very positive connection to Dragons dating back to his days as a young wizard in Wales. He understood the sacred relevance of Dragons, their longevity and skin-shedding renewal making them symbols of eternal life. Naturally, this did not jibe with the new faith, which preferred to see Merlin and his draconic cohorts as anything from inconvenient plot points to servants of the devil.[38]

For Christians, eternal life resided in the grace of accepting Jesus of Nazareth as one's savior and in the Holy Grail as his vital instrument sent forth to inspire and heal the world—literally. King Pelles knew this grace: he was a descendant of Joseph of Arimathea, best known as the man who donated his own tomb for Jesus's burial (Malory's link between the Dragon in a "tomb" and the tomb of Jesus is too obvious to be anything but deliberate) and keeper of the Grail. Yet in Arthurian Britain, that was not enough. To defeat the old beliefs, Malory needed to tap the chivalric code of might for right and employ the sword of the best (though imperfect) knight in the land. Once the Dragon's defeated, the Grail is free to appear before the king and his champion once more, the Eternal Divine in the mortal world.

---

38. To accommodate these sensibilities, Malory takes Merlin out of the picture early in Book IV, allowing the new faith to flourish with only a few Dragons left to be fought and reviled. *Le Morte d'Arthur*, 69–70.

Hand in hand with this, the Dragon represents the era's physical dangers that plagued the lawful ruler (state) of Pointe Corbyn and his people. It was common knowledge, after all, that Dragons could be very destructive, especially if cornered or under siege. (There is practical truth to the adage, "More fool he who wakes the Dragon.") And finally, the Dragon is a barrier between Elaine the Maid and Elaine the Woman, Mother of Galahad, the Perfect Knight. Even though Launcelot was duped into believing he was bedding Gwynevere at the time, he would not have been in a position to bed anyone had he not gone through the Dragon first. As such, the creature represents the threshold into adulthood: the natural spontaneity of youth which must be conquered so that a spiritual hero can be born.

Thus, without so much as a draconic by-your-leave, Malory burdened this one poor Dragon with all the conflict of the age.

Spenser's Dragon in The Faërie Queene

Renaissance Dragons continued, at least superficially, in the mold of their medieval counterparts; they were the monstrous face of evil in the world, the test of valor, manhood, and Christian righteousness. This was the age of allegory in which romance was laced with religion and then tumbled down the slippery slope into politics and humanism. Dragons, familiar to all and burdened by symbolism that dated back a millennium, were tailor-made for this sort of narrative. They danced through Dante's fourteenth-century *Divine Comedy* and Ludovico Ariosto's 1516 *Orlando Furioso*, and even enlivened the wicked sixteenth-century satires of François Rabelais. But these were Dragons as two-dimensional supporting players at best, their creators relying on the reader's everyday experience to flesh out rather unimaginative portraits. Ariosto was more intrigued by his hero Orlando's demented journey to love, for example, than the lives of the Dragons he encountered along the way.

Then there was the English poet Edmund Spenser (c. 1552–99), allegorist *par excellence*, who knew Dragons with a fierce intimacy none of his contemporaries could touch. Inspired by Ariosto, Spenser's epic masterpiece, *The Faërie Queene*, is an intricate story of politics and religion dressed in the fanciful trappings of knights and ladies in the land of the Faë. No such tale would be complete without a Dragon, and, on that score, Spenser does not disappoint.

Book I follows the very unsmooth path to true love of the Lady Una and the Redcrosse Knight, who is virtue personified and is later revealed to be St. George. The Knight is pledged to the service of the Faërie Queene, Gloriana:

> *To proue his puissance in battell braue…*
> *Vpon his foe, a Dragon horrible and stearne.*[39]

After a host of trials and deceptions, Una and her champion come at last to her father's realm and the draconic encounter unfolds. Despite the rightness of the human cause, the Dragon holds the upper paw for two days. Twice Redcrosse is beaten back, near death, only to rise new-born through divine intervention: first he tumbles into the Well of Life, then he is healed by a balm from the Tree of Life— the same tree some say was, ironically, guarded by a Dragon in Eden. Finally, on the third day, stronger than ever thanks

---

39. Spenser, *Faërie Queene*, 41.

to the blessings of pure faith, he runs the Dragon through. Anthems of thanks are raised and just rewards meted out: knight and fair lady are betrothed and, in time (Redcrosse still had six year's service owed to the Faërie Queene), all live happily ever after.

On the surface, this seems not unlike your standard medieval adventure story. Evil Dragon meets his demise, king rewards knight with his daughter's hand. But in allegories, it all comes down to who or what your characters represent. On one level, this is a basic good versus evil story: Redcrosse is Holiness, Una ("The One") is Sacred Truth, and the Dragon is Satan, who stands in the way of their union. But let us remember the tumultuous political/religious environment of the times. It was the early years of the Protestant Reformation (1517–1648). Catholic kingdoms like Spain and France curried favor with the Vatican by setting their military sights on England and her heretic monarch, Elizabeth I (1533–1603). They failed. The Ridolfi Plot intent upon assassinating Elizabeth and putting Mary, Queen of Scots on the British throne was foiled in 1570, and the Spanish Armada defeated in 1588. Against this backdrop—the first part of the *The Faërie Queene* was published in 1590—Spenser created a poetic universe that was a hymn to the Virgin Queen and the rightness of her reign. Gloriana the Faërie Queene is Elizabeth I, and Redcrosse represents her good Christian subjects in the personage of St. George. Holy champion of the realm, he risks life and limb defending the "true" Anglican Church (Una) against the "false" Catholic Church (the Dragon of the Papacy). The defeat of the Dragon, close call though it was, celebrates England's victory against papal plots, great and small, and Queen Elizabeth as the rightful defender of the true faith.

But let's return to the Dragon. Despite the creature's less than savory character and ultimate demise, Spenser took great care to provide more than a cardboard cutout of evil—so much care that it's clear he was not only familiar with Dragons but, one might venture, a bit of a fan. The first glimpse we get of this magnificent creature is positively idyllic: he is basking on a hillside, his very presence more than enough to imprison king and court within the castle. Roused by the sun reflecting off of the knight's armor, the Dragon attacks, "halfe flying, and halfe footing in his hast," his "woundrous greatnesse ... swolne with wrath, & poyson, & with bloudy gore."[40] Ranging across eight stanzas, Spenser, although making free use of poetic license to shape the belief system of his tale, proceeds to draw one of the most detailed draconic portraits in literature. From plated scales to saber talons, fiery eyes to deadly jaws, he presents a creature teeming with awe-inspiring glory. He is a goliath, with wings so vast that when he beats the air ...

> *The cloudes before him fled in terror great,*
> *And all the heavens stood still amazed with his threat.*
> *His huge long tayle wound up in hundred foldes,*
> *Does ouerspread his long bras-scaly backe ...*
> *But his most hideous head my toung to tell,*
> *Does tremble: for his deepe deuouring iawes,*
> *Wide gaped, like the grisly mouth of hell ....*[41]

40. Spenser, *Faërie Queene*, 180.
41. Ibid., 180–81.

And when this mountain of a being falls, the ground ripples beneath Redcrosse's feet, just as the fall of papal authority sent ripples through the Christian world. This was a proper Dragon, a proper challenge, roaring through the Renaissance and lending fierce authority to Spenser's epic work.

Renaissance Dragons and the Visual Arts

It would be remiss to discuss Renaissance Dragons without looking at how they were portrayed by the visual artists of the age. In contrast to Spenser's fully realized, quasi-naturalistic Dragon, most of the old masters took a more restrained— one might say whimsical and/or ill-informed—approach. From the Flemish painter Rogier van der Weyden (1399– 1464) to the Italian masters Raphael (1483–1520) and Vittore Carpaccio (1465–1526), the conservative (i.e., religious) artists of the day held tight to the notion of the Dragon as a hideous, evil monster to be skewered by heroic angel or saint. Though less stylized than the medieval and Byzantine artists before them, it is clear to even novice dracophiles that Renaissance masters could not tell a Welsh gwiber from an Irish peiste. Artistically stunning though the paintings are, such ignorance means they do little for our understanding of Dragons or their ways.

This was particularly evident in depictions of Saints George, Michael, Margaret, et al., and their draconic foes. Despite a neoclassical focus on anatomy, nature, and the resulting realism thereof, these doomed creatures were usually small—certainly smaller than your average steed—and often bipedal. Carpaccio's St. George, for example, confronts a creature that, though equipped with the proper number of limbs, is little more than 3 feet tall at the shoulder and looks more like a lion with wings than a proper Dragon.[42] Hardly the great behemoths of legend nor naturalistic Spenserian titans, the miniature size of these painted creatures demeaned our friends and inadvertently knocked some of the awesomeness out of their sainted slayers. A Dragon little bigger than a mastiff was vulnerable to staff-wielding villagers, so who needed a well-armed knight with God on his side? Of course, this was brushed aside by arguments that the threat is not in the size of the creature but in its nature: Dragons, being in league with the devil, were as bad-natured as they come.

This misrepresentation had practical effects as well. Anyone who got their draconic education from the artistic masters and rode out expecting to find the wilderness populated by stunted Dragons would be greatly, even disastrously, surprised. Imagine the dread they'd experience upon seeing a pair of full-grown Ardennes whiptails—60 feet from stem to stern—stalking trout in France's Semois River! Trembling right out of their doublets and cross-gartered hose is a distinct possibility.

There are exceptions to every rule, and Venetian painter Tintoretto's (1518–94) *Saint George and the Dragon* does show a True Dragon that, though not full grown, is certainly large enough to give one pause. Unfortunately, this small painting was intended for a private parlor and is, as such, of limited educational value. However, it is currently on display at London's National Gallery.

If the religious artists were underwhelming with their Dragons, the Humanists more than made amends in their

---

42. See Vittore Carpaccio's *St. George and the Dragon*, Scuola di San Giorgio degli Schiavoni, Venice.

portraits of legendary Dragons. Paintings of Greek tales like Perseus rescuing Andromeda and Jason stealing the Golden Fleece include creatures of great size and fanciful form, conjured from extremely inventive imaginations. Through the center of Piero di Cosimo's 1515 *Perseus Freeing Andromeda* wades a great tusked-and-maned sea dragon that looks remarkably like a cross between the apalala (a massive water dragon from India) and a tusked North American gowrow. This cross-culturalism is not as strange as it sounds: two hundred years previously, Marco Polo returned from China with Dragon tales in tow,[43] and the New World was being explored in di Cosimo's lifetime. Though gowrow habitat is currently limited to remote corners of Arkansas's Ozark and Ouachita Mountains, five hundred years ago their range could well have stretched from the southern Atlantic coast to what is today eastern Oklahoma.

Curiously, one of the most fantastic and allegorical painters of the age, Hieronymus Bosch (1450–1516), a man familiar with griffins, unicorns, flying fish, even horned leopards, worked very little with Dragons. True, there is one tiny, rather standard Dragon swimming in a moat in the background of his *Temptation of St. Anthony*, but not so much as a glimmer of them in his most famous piece, *The Garden of Earthly Delights*, not even in Hell. Cryptoherpetologists and cutting-edge art historians have come to the conclusion that Bosch, an observant naturalist, must have been acquainted with his native Dutch Dragons, their forms and habits. However, comfortable though he might have been putting three heads

---

43. Da Vinci made sketches for a Dragon costume which was 100 percent Asian, right down to his serpentine body, leonine mane, and whiskers.

on a peacock, insulting the enchantments with demonic caricatures—even for the greater glory of God—would have gone beyond the pale.

Faërie Tales and Fantasy: Toward a Modern Dragon Aesthetic

As a literary genre, faërie tales did not appear until the late seventeenth century. It was then that French authors Charles Perrault (1628–1703) and Madame d'Aulnoy (1650–1705) penned the first official *contes de fees*, or stories of the faëries. These first tales were collected and adapted from the vibrant oral tradition of hearth-side yarns and bedtime entertainments; by being written down, they acquired a permanent place in the human psyche.

One should know from the start that, despite their timeless lineage, faërie tales should not be confused with legends or lore, especially where Dragons are concerned. Lore and legend have ties to the natural and physical sciences; faërie tales, at their essence, are flights of fancy. Lore and legend are cultural and societal in their influence and laced with heavy doses of religion; faërie tales are personal and deeply psychological and leave religion by the wayside. With magic, gore, and wonder, they teach us lessons needed for life in the real world. They lead us by the hand into the woods—or the Dragon's lair—so that we might push the envelope of our existence and come out the other side stronger, wiser, and more fully ourselves. Wild and dangerous, the air singing with experience and paths overgrown with passion and fear, this is the Kingdom of the Faërie. Even as they became harder to find in the real world than a zebra at the Ritz, Dragons were right at home.

In the enchantment-rich realm of faërie tales, anything is possible and things are seldom as they seem. Beasts can be as beautiful as the fairest rose and beauties as foul as the rankest carrion. Dragons play all the roles: white hat, black hat, and every shade in between. Muscles pulsing with life, fangs and claws laden with death, they're guardians of hidden treasure, dispensers of justice, and humans in disguise.

This last was always problematic. While turning someone into a Dragon seems, at first blush, a powerful punishment (Dragons would consider it a reward, of course), in reality the molecular differences between Dragon and human are such that even the strongest sorcerer's spell would last two weeks, tops. There is some speculation that the more attuned a person is to their internal Dragon the longer such magic might last. C. S. Lewis (1898–1963) toyed with this idea in the Narnia book *The Voyage of the Dawn Treader*, when Eustace's selfish and surly disposition turned him dragonish for a seeming eternity. Of course, Eustace was a better boy with the Narnians as a Dragon than he ever was with them as a boy. Only when he learned how to be truly human was he able to see the divine lion, Aslan, and shed his Dragon skin.

In the land of the faërie, Dragons reclaimed their majesty, at last becoming life size (sometimes larger), full of fire and bluster, and with natures as unpredictable as they were wild. What sort of Dragon lurked around the corner? Would he be a ravenous eating machine or a benevolent dispenser of wit and counsel? Perhaps he'd airlift the hero over the next mountain to battle ogres—it could happen. And it was just this uncertainty, combined with the natural aspects of the species, that gave them new layers and intrigue. True, in most faërie tales, Dragons were depicted as solitary creatures, a fact which explains much when it comes to their often antisocial personalities. If the authors of such stories were inspired by local rogues, their accounts of edgy, even hostile, behavior would have verged on scientific truth. Dragons are community-oriented beings, so isolation is usually the result of some terrible disaster or grief; being solitary makes a Dragon vulnerable, which in turn makes them hyper-vigilant and fairly mean.

Koschei the Deathless

Even when cast as faërie-tale villains, Dragons were rarely caricatures. The Slavic story of Koschei the Deathless One is a perfect example of this. Koschei was one of the great villains of all time, a being who appeared as everything from a wicked old man to a fleshless skeleton. And in some Russian tales, he was a Dragon; naturally, this is the persona that interests us here. It is said Koschei was in cahoots with the legendary Baba Yaga, who made him immortal by taking his soul from his body and hiding it far away inside an egg—inside a duck, inside a hare, inside a crystal coffer—and buried it beneath an oak on an island far out in the sea. While Baba Yaga is seen as Crone, Wise Woman, or terrifying witch depending on her mood and whom you talk to, there's little dispute over the Dragon's character: Koschei is thoroughly unpleasant, his wickedness varying by mere degrees from tale to tale.

The quintessential Koschei story involves a stolen princess, a hero's quest, and death to the Deathless One, an act even die-hard dracophiles would view as self-defense. Once upon a time, the great Dragon tires of gathering mere gold and gems and, seeking a treasure beyond compare, absconds with the most beautiful maiden in all the Russias. As beautiful maidens often are, this one was a princess, and she needed a hero. No one knows for sure, but it is often reported that the fabled warrior, Bulat the Brave, stepped up to the task, putting brain before brawn as he searched the world over for the egg in which the Dragon's soul was hidden. Smashing it against Koschei's bony head—recombining body and spirit—Bulat slew the creature and saved the fair damsel.

Fortunately not all Koschei-esque tales go to such extremes. "The Dragon and His Grandmother"[44] is such a story. Here you find a cunningly fiendish Dragon that makes a bargain with three young deserters from the Tsar's army. He gives them a magic whip that—*crack!*—provides them with unlimited wealth and all the status and pleasure it can buy. At the end of seven years' time, they must repay the Dragon with their eternal servitude. Of course, there is always an escape clause in faërie tales: if the trio is able to answer the Dragon's riddle, their contract will become null and void. Seven years of high living draw to a close, and two of the men start dreading their covenant with the Dragon, pulling their scalps bald at the prospect of serving him for the rest of their days. But the third remains annoyingly cheerful, convinced he will guess the riddle with ease. An old woman passes by and offers them aid: "One of you," she says, "must go into the woods and enter a rocky ruin, there you will find the help you need." With predictable faërie-tale idiocy, the two sullen fellows dismiss the old woman's

---

44. Lang, *The Yellow Fairy Book*. Koschei is not mentioned by name, but the parallels are undeniable.

advice out of hand, but the joyful one bounds off into the woods and finds the ruined house. Inside lives a wizened old woman who just happens to be the Dragon's grand-mother—Baba Yaga in one of her more benign aspects. Captivated by the young man and his story, she tells him not to worry. Her grandson is coming by for dinner, and after some borscht, latkas, and a flagon of wine, any Dragon is apt to turn chatty. She will lure him into revealing the answer to his riddle while the youth eavesdrops behind the cellar door. A Dragon may be clever, but a Dragon's grandmother is always more so. Events play out according to plan: in the usual manner of riddling tales, human charm and guile triumph, and the Dragon is thwarted. With a fervid roar, he wings off into the night, living to flimflam another day.

A word about Dragons and the law: Faërie tales play fast and loose with the basic tenets of contract law, with "heroes" being rewarded not for keeping their word but for being trickier than the other guy. For all the slurs flung their way, Dragons know the rules of give and take and will always pay the piper. That humans try to back out of uncomfortable agreements after years of reaping their benefits speaks to our view of honor; that Dragons don't just up and eat us when we trick them out of their compensation speaks to theirs.

The Black Dragon and the Red Dragon

The global scope of faërie tales makes their land of origin as important to a Dragon's presentation as anything else. Indeed, while European traditions kept Dragons rather antagonistic, their natures mellow as one travels east, befitting the regard with which they're held in Asia. So it is from

Turkey that we have the tale of "The Black Dragon and the Red Dragon."[45] Long, long ago, we are told, there was a Turkish king, a Padishah, who was surely the most ill-fated man in all Anatolia. He had forty children, all beautiful and loved, and all stolen from him when they reached their seventh birthdays. No one in the whole world knew such grief! How could they? He was the king, and his children were the best and the brightest! One night his royal loss became more than he could bear; pulling his despair tight about him, he walked out into the desert. As J. R. R. Tolkien wrote, "Not all those who wander are lost." Sometimes we are just seeking. And sometimes, when the night of the soul is as starless as a black hole, wandering is the universe's way of shaking us up, opening our eyes, and returning us to the light.

In the course of the Padishah's trek, he goes from pitiful to strong, shattered to whole, thanks in no small part to the wisdom of two remarkable beings: the Black Dragon and her brother, the Red Dragon. They not only help him find his children but make him a better king in the process. In details as intricate as a Byzantine arabesque, this is a story about families, love and loss, and setting things right. It is about the similarities between us—even Dragons and humans—rather than the differences. The self-absorbed Padishah of the beginning of the story would never have thought creatures, let alone Dragons, could love their children as much as he did. Yet when the Black Dragon lost her newborn brood, the painfully maternal lament she loosed across the mountains broke even the hardest heart. Family

---

45. Kúnos, *Forty-Four Turkish Fairy Tales.*

is family and grief is grief, as anyone with more than a passing acquaintance with Dragons knows.

Touched—and not a little fearful—the Padishah shows respect in the face of power and relates how he'd recently crossed paths with a host of infant Dragons. Their eyes were still closed (poetic license, here, as Dragons are born with their eyes open), so they stumbled blindly around the desert, unable to find their way home. Cautiously optimistic that this is her lost brood, the Black Dragon flies off and, lo, the king was right! There her children are, huddled together, frightened and forlorn. She herds them home and then, as is only fair, she and her brother help the human rescue his stolen children. (Who had been spirited away by the evil Peri and transformed into birds. At least that's what a dervish told the king in a dream.)

In the end, the Padishah learns and triumphs. He returns to his palace wiser and more compassionate for his adventures. The lost are found, justice is done; there is dancing, laughter, and even forgiveness where it is due. In the happily-ever-after way of these things, one likes to believe the Padishah issued an edict banning Dragon hunting in perpetuity. It would have been the right thing to do.

Modern Fantasy

The quantum leap in draconic understanding evidenced in tales like "The Black Dragon and the Red Dragon" broke down the barriers between the species and propelled us into no-holds-barred modern fantasy. Modern fantasy is literature's uncharted territory in which "Here there be Dragons!" is about the only thing a reader can expect with any degree of certainty.

With leathery sails spread upon the wind and flames slicing across clouds, the Dragons who fill fantastical skies are beings more wondrous than any of their aesthetic forerunners, and for good reason: as a genre, fantasy developed alongside the nineteenth-century Neo-Druids and the Pre-Raphaelite Brotherhood—a group of writers and artists influenced by medievalism and the spiritual. Their passionate belief in Dragons was instrumental in calling our scaly friends back from the misty realms on a wing and a flare. Add to that advances in natural and crypto sciences—not to mention an increasing number of firsthand encounters—and centuries of misleading portraits were suddenly being redrawn with breathtaking reality. Nothing grounds fabulous fiction quite like the authority gained from writing what one knows, and the Dragons celebrated in modern literature are known down to the last polished cornicle (nose-horn) and raggedy dewclaw. Unlike their predecessors, modern fantasists know not to call a basilisk a gwiber and that a hydra has only two heads (unless of course they are writing historical fantasy and referencing the nine-headed Lernaean Hydra of Herculean fame). Dragon-savvy audiences know these things, too—or can discover them with a quick Internet search—thus demanding more accuracy than ever before.

Not that artistic license isn't taken. Fantasy isn't nonfiction, after all. However, such liberties are more often taken in matters of temperament than physique. The character of these creatures has an elaborate pedigree, being indebted to a host of nineteenth-century influences, from folklorists Jacob and Wilhelm Grimm to American Transcendentalists like Henry David Thoreau and Ralph Waldo

Emerson, from Lewis Carroll to the twentieth-century Sigmund Freud, making them aggregates of the very best sort. "It's a metaphor of human bloody existence, a dragon," Terry Pratchett explained. "And if that wasn't bad enough, it's also a bloody great hot flying thing." These Dragons are wild and tame, destroyers of kingdoms and saviors of worlds. They indulge our longing for the freedom of flight and our delusion of invincibility. Silent or chatty, patient or petulant, they are high-altitude Moby-Dicks and weyr-dwelling Yodas, mirroring the best and worst of the people around them. In short, like all characters, they serve the pleasure of the author.

True, fantasy pioneers cast most Dragons in rather traditional and unflattering roles. Case in point: J. R. R. Tolkien (1892–1973) and his tales of Middle Earth, *The Lord of the Rings*, *The Hobbit*, and so on. Though he said as a child he "desired dragons with a profound desire,"[46] as an adult Tolkien used our friends sparingly and always on the wrong side of the good fight. Glaurung and Smaug, the greatest Dragons of their age, are ill-tempered if cagey creatures, with no compunctions about protecting their vast hoards with fire, fang, or "dragon-spell." And, with a feather versus scale bias, the nameless Fell Beasts fly the evil Witch King and his Nazgûl into battle, while the heroes—Gandalf, Elves, Dwarves, and Hobbits—soar astride the Great Eagles. (It should also be noted that the eagles are given names—Thorondor, Gwaihir, etc.—and, thus, specific personalities, whereas the Fell Beasts are not.)

---

46. Tolkein, *On Fairy-Stories*, 14.

Naturally, some aficionados of the fantasy genre insist this is the only proper role for a Dragon to play: the bigger and badder the better, preferably with lots of people-eating thrown in for good measure. These readers consider anything less than monstrous, rampaging killers to be as ineffectual as pygmy chameleons. Looking back, one sees this attitude as fueled more by a love of epic conflict than draconic fact. Still, for a time, this meant "good" Dragons were restricted to children's books—reminders of our innocence when we saw Dragons in all their wonder, even envied them a little—or, as in C. S. Lewis's science-fiction novel *Perelandra,* to tales set in other worlds, where conventional notions of good, evil, and requisite mortal combat need not apply.

As fantasy literature grew up, so did the Dragons in its midst. From scene-stealing extras to lead players, they were everywhere, flourishing metaphors able to encompass both our darkest fears and noblest ambitions without a hint of irony or contradiction. After all, their wildness made them unconventional and their physical attributes made them dangerous. Their intellect, experiences, and affections were the x-factors that shaped them one way or another. The Dragons populating Ursula Le Guin's island realm of Earthsea, for example, are masters of wandering the middle road, due in large part to their complicated relationship with the local wizards—particularly Ged, Dragonlord, and Archmage. Here's a hero who, on his journey from farm lad to great wizard, interacts with numerous Dragons. He comes to see them as the complex creatures they are and treat them accordingly: with respect and caution. To Ged's benefit and delight, they return the courtesy.[47] As an old man, he can say without doubt that

> *though I came to forget or regret all I have ever done,*
> *yet would I remember that once I saw the dragons aloft*
> *on the wind at sunset above the western isles; and I*
> *would be content.*[48]

Where to turn from here? We all have our favorites, characters who speak one-on-one to our inner dracophile. There is Terry Pratchett's Machiavellian Dragon in *Guards! Guards!*; the Dragons "mothered" by Daenerys Targaryen in George R. R. Martin's epic *A Game of Thrones*; and on the lighter side, J. Bissell-Thomas's titular Dragon Green, a being with so much Romeo in his soul that he wins the heart of a princess and convinces her to join him in Dragonhood. The list is as long as a Dragon's tail, for what self-respecting scrivener hasn't flirted with Dragons? (See the recommended reading list at the end of this book, for a start.)

Yet no look at modern literary Dragons would be complete without at least mentioning the noble fliers of Anne McCaffrey's multi-volume saga set on the planet Pern. Some say McCaffrey's heroic weyr inhabitants are fantasy, yet they are more aptly the product of an intricate science-fiction universe, an elegant technological solution to a dire scientific problem. When the colonists on Pern are assaulted by the all-consuming Thread falling from the Red Star, they need a way to fight it or perish. Using advanced technology, a geneticist mutates indigenous fire-lizards—

---

47. See Ursula K. Le Guin, *The Earthsea Trilogy*.
48. Ibid., *The Farthest Shore*, 37.

miniature draconic creatures domesticated for pets—into full grown, fire-breathing dragons. With their human riders, these great beings combat the Thread and save the world of Pern.

Though inspired by the Dragons of Earth, the Pernese creatures are a definite breed apart. They are smooth-skinned, not scaled, with an equine aspect derived from their fire-lizard forebears. They are also telepathic, able to converse with the each other and their people at will. With genetically engineered bonds to their riders that will override even instincts of self-preservation, they are the ultimate "good" Dragons—so good, in fact, that some dracophiles have suggested they are not Dragons at all. They are too subservient, they say; too much kitten, not enough tiger. They are used like war horses, but worse, because they have keen intelligence but no free will. This, of course, emphasizes that we're talking fiction here, not fact—and, as we've seen from the start, creative minds do what they will with Dragons. What such critics ignore is that the dragons of Pern are more true to life than not in many ways, particularly in their social structure and ability to bond with humans.

Cryptoherpetologists may argue the fine points but, in the end, we welcome any tale that sparks interest in our friends outside of damsel-eating mode, treating them not as remnants of a faërie-tale past but as flesh-and-blood forces in a scientific present and future. Though taken to literary extremes, there can be little doubt that personal acquaintance with—and true affection for—Dragons infuses McCaffrey's work. For that, all dracophiles should be grateful.[49]

The aesthetic of Dragons continues to shift around us, directly reflecting our understanding of their species as well as the growth of our own. With each new incarnation, they have more range, humor, and humanity than before, reminding us that, as much as art lends truth to life, so Dragons give truth to art.

Tellers of tales hold these Dragons dear for their passion, humor, and humanity, hoping, as poet Rainer Maria Rilke wrote in *Letters to a Young Poet*,

> *that perhaps all the dragons of our lives are princesses who are only waiting to see us once beautiful and brave. Perhaps everything terrible is in its deepest being something helpless that wants help from us.*

---

49. See Anne McCaffrey's *The Dragonriders of Pern* and *Dragonsdawn*, to name a few.

Part III

Living with Dragons

nine

In the World

J. R. R. Tolkien was wiser than he knew when he wrote in *The Hobbit*, "It does not do to leave a live dragon out of your calculations, if you live near him."

Of course, if it was up to them, most Dragons wouldn't live near us at all. Alas, that is not the way of the modern world. Humans have invaded virtually every square inch of the land, and we're fast working on the seas. It is only natural that we are running into Dragons right, left, and center. The safety and care of Dragons—and humans, too—in this modern Venn-diagram intersection requires a whole new skill set for naturalists around the world.

Sanctuaries

On the surface, much of living with Dragons seems a matter of common sense, especially when discussing environment. Just as you can't raise a llama in a Manhattan brownstone, you can't raise a Dragon there either, so don't even try. (Granted, some of the smaller household dragons—pisuhänds and aitvaras—while preferring rural habitats, can be found most anywhere, but they are the exception, not the rule.) In fact, for the vast majority of dracophiles, it is best not to raise Dragons at all—but more on that in Chapter 10. It is a no-brainer that our friends need open skies, clean waters, and lots of room. They also need a ready and diverse source of ingestibles: animal, vegetable, and mineral. While the occasional sighting does occur within city limits, nine times out of ten, they are vacationing Dragons briefly resting atop a skyscraper or taking in the sights of our glass-and-steel jungles. The increased designation of no-fly zones over major Western cities has cut the number of such visitations considerably over the past decade—not that they couldn't fly under the radar if they understood what it was. So, if you come across a Dragon basking in Paris's Jardins des Tuileries, be sure to take a picture. Chances are you'll not see her like again.

It goes without saying that the best place to run into a Dragon is at one of the growing number of WAFDE-approved sanctuaries. That is, the World Association for Dragons Everywhere, the heart and soul of the Dragon Conservancy Program. Not as flashy as Apollo's Garden of Epirotes (see page 119), modern sanctuaries are closer to the model put forth by national parks and wildlife preserves: vast integrated ecosystems encompassing weyrs around the world. Under strict supervision (which is as much for your safety as the Dragons') and for a reasonable fee, dracophiles can explore the sanctuaries via guided photo safaris. They are also excellent open laboratories for research. Dragons can be observed in their natural habitats, interacting in a safe and relaxed manner, as free from human interference as is possible in today's world. Of course, nothing is perfect: miles of porous borders mean poachers can enter sanctuary lands. That said, Dragons are as well equipped to deal with them as any creature on the endangered lists, and sanctuaries have proved *the* instrumental factor in advancing Dragon sciences over the past fifty years.

Sanctuaries are also integral to the Adopt-A-Dragon (AAD) Program, a public outreach project that allows people to learn about Dragons, get close to them, and contribute to their well-being in the process. Using a model similar to the World Wildlife Fund's adopt-an-animal initiatives, AAD is able to funnel all funds raised back into enchantment conservation. A recent offshoot is Kids For Dragons (KFD), a program geared at students from the sixth grade—first form, for our British friends—on up. Understandably, Dragons are considered a little too terrifying for very young children; there are enough obstacles to our friends' well-being without adding irate parents and the clamor of the psychiatric community to the mix. With parental consent, school groups can pool their resources and adopt a young Dragon. The charge is nominal and AAD tries to hook classes up with Dragons from nearby sanctuaries to facilitate visitations. As a scientific teaching tool and dispeller of negative PR, the program is without equal! Nothing beats going to see the class adoptee for field trips, watching her grow through the years from gangly Dragonlet to full-winged, fire-breathing adolescent. If you or your school are interested in partaking in all KFD has to offer, contact your local chapter of WAFDE.

Backyard Visitors

While sanctuaries are the most accessible means of safely associating with enchantments, some Dragon aficionados seek more intimate connections. This longing for less-restrictive interaction—combined with the fact that there is no fence high enough to hold a Dragon with wanderlust—has led to an elaborate network of Dragon lay-bys, or rest stops, around the globe.

Naturally, if you wish to entice Dragons into your neck of the woods, the first thing you need is woods—at least forty-plus acres of lush and varied wilderness, capable of providing all the creature comforts: fresh water, shelter, and victuals both flora and fauna. Next, know your Dragons. This means doing your homework and boning up on the specific needs of Dragons indigenous to your region as well as those likely to pass through. To this end, do not be afraid to ask questions, especially of WAFDE or the cryptozoology department at your local college (if they have one). Recent years have seen a remarkable lay-by building boom in the Sun Belt—from southern Utah right through Baja California and Mexico's Chihuahuan Desert highlands. This is less indicative of population growth among desert weyrs and more of an increase in visitors from cooler climes. After all, who doesn't like a little vacation in the sun? Naturally, this places special demands on the lay-by provider, especially in terms of extra water and relief from the elements. Though desert Dragons can survive the blazing sun and aridity of their environments, these factors can be extremely dangerous to those not so well adapted. One must think in terms of creating lush oases, with deep pools and shelters cooled by the prevailing winds.

Those of you who get queasy at the thought of voracious predators hunting through your back forty might as well stop here. You'll obviously be happier keeping Dragons as long-distance acquaintances. There is no way around the fact that Dragons are omnivores with enthusiastic appetites, and this gets messy. Fish—the gutting of which, for reasons past understanding, seems to bother humans less than cuddlier wildlife—serve well enough as day-to-day fare, making a well-stocked lake or stream key to a good lay-by. However, the energy expended by long flights requires high caloric intake only red-blooded meat can provide; one way or another, fur will fly. Animal lovers can be comforted by the fact there is give as well as take, here: in the off-season, many properly planned Dragons rests serve as wildlife refuges where deer, pheasant, raccoons, and such retreat to avoid hunters.

Despite being raised for consumption, domestic livestock should be offered only as a last resort. The meat is too fatty and educates their palates in ways that will only get Dragons into trouble down the line. Take the occasional wolf crossing out of Yellowstone into ranch land, multiply the resultant hysteria by a thousand, and you might get a glimmer of the wrath that would be directed at enchantments who develop a taste for cattle. Likewise, do not "tame" (by way of feeding stands and such) any wildlife who might later wind up a Dragon delicacy. Aside from it being bad form, remember that Dragons are hunters. The thrill of the chase gives the prey a fighting chance and stimulates draconic appetites.

Dragons relish vegetation in its infinite variety. They will eat shoots and leaves and snack on everything from fruit to nuts with fungi on the side. Careful planting and replanting can greatly enhance the allure of a lay-by. Keep in mind native species, color (bright flowers are particularly appetizing), taste, as well as elemental balance.[50] Dragons enjoy occasional treats of garden veggies, especially peppers and members of the nightshade family (tomatoes, eggplant, etc.), and in times of extreme drought or during hard winters, supplements of sweet hay will not go unappreciated. The one thing to absolutely stay clear of are natural hallucinogens: peyote, amanita, psilocybin, and deliriants such as mandrake and datura (jimson weed). Though they can tolerate the toxins well enough, young/adolescent Dragons have been known to experience the mind-altering properties of these plants with dangerous abandon if they are ingested in sufficient quantities. (On a sociological note, the Dragon grapevine has been buzzing with reports of a recently discovered monograph by Carlos Castaneda, "Flight of the Vision Serpent: Feathered Dragons and Psychotropic Plants of the Mexican Plateau." History tells us the shamans of the regions were long wise in the ways of both Feathered Dragons and psychotropics, yet, much as the rumor intrigues, for the time

---

50. If you're garden challenged, Scott Cunningham's *Encyclopedia of Magical Herbs*, Sandra Kynes' *Whispers from the Woods*, and your local horticultural college are great places to start.

being it remains just that: a rumor. Cryptoherpetologists are following developments with skeptical interest.)

Finally, minerals are essential to draconic well-being. From salts (sodium and magnesium) to flint chips for fire, calcium for bones, and iron and copper for their blood, Dragons need them all. Most are found in the game and plants they eat, though mineral licks are welcome, especially in warmer climes.

Able to weather the most inclement storms, Dragons nonetheless appreciate rocky caverns or overhangs for shelter and privacy. Pits of fine sand are perfect for dust-baths, a welcome alternative to water as well an anti-parasite treatment second only to shedding. (Parasites are not a bother for full-grown Dragons, as their hides are impenetrable to the meanest tick or louse. Young Dragons and pseudo-dragons relish a good dust-out between the scales.) Scatter about a few granite boulders for burnishing horns ("charming") and your visitors will feel right at home.

Once a lay-by is set up, it must be inspected and licensed by WAFDE. This guarantees everything is up to snuff and carries with it full rights and privileges of WAFDE membership. Display your credentials publically; hoist the WAFDE standard proudly! You are now part of the respected lay-by system. This network also provides a foundation for scientists studying enchantment migratory and vacation patterns. Flight corridors, like those skirting New England's Long Trail or running from the Welsh highlands to France's Massif Central, have already been mapped in detail, but with an increase in Dragon-friendly nooks in unexpected places, it is anyone's guess where future avenues of interaction will arise. Of growing concern is the fact that while

Dragon rests are most active from late spring through mid-summer, an alarming number of polar Dragons—known for surviving bitter, sub-zero weather—have been sighted below the Tropic of Cancer in recent winters. The ecological implications here are still being examined.

The WAFDE is also collecting empirical data on the most attractive lay-by layouts and seasonal/regional plantings. Cryptozoologists likewise treasure the growing wealth of information on inter-weyr behavior, information they'd be hard pressed to get without the benefit of the network maintained by dedicated civilian dracophiles. For example, *pax loci* (peace of the place)—the unspoken way in which sojourning Dragons treat shared space as sacred and inviolate—was considered one of the great myths of enchantment lore until verified by lay-by observations. In short, what is a private delight for lay-by providers is a public boon for cryptoherpetologists around the world.

A note about Dragons and pets: Be careful, especially with dogs. While Dragons respect wolves, foxes, and their wild ilk, they have a low tolerance for domesticated canines. This is believed to be a throwback to the dark days of Dragon slaying when packs were used to hound and harry Dragons from their weyrs. Of course, it might also be a simple clash of personalities, Dragons being more attuned to independent-minded felines and small mammals (too small to make a good meal, of course) than cloying pups. If you have dogs, be sure to keep them under control and on a leash until all parties get used to one another. And always remember you are dealing with *wild* Dragons: as approachable as they may seem, they are a dangerous law unto themselves.

Summoning Dragons

After you have constructed your lay-by, be patient. One season you may only see the occasional flier overhead, scouting out the environment. The next year, you might actually get a drop-in or two. Bit by bit, word will get out, and seven, eight years down the line, if you have done your work well (and are not too out-of-the-way), you should have regular company from May to September. At first blush, location often seems more important to success than high-class features. Build on an established route and you will likely have Dragons on your doorstep within a year. If you are off the beaten path, you may have to wait for an adventurous lone soul in need of a safe place to unwind. But, just as with that gem of a B&B nestled in a village miles from the Interstate, in the end, excellence counts. Though you may not be inundated with Dragons, chances are you will get a core group of repeat patrons for whom quality trumps convenience (and the overcrowding that often comes with it).

Despite the fact that working with Dragons is an inherently long-term endeavor, some people are looking at ways to speed up the process and actually call Dragons out of the skies. Since Dragons are vocal creatures, using sound for summoning seems a sensible approach. Logically one thinks of electronic replication of Dragonsong, but this has proved problematic. Like whales, Dragons weave intricate, generational melodies. We can only guess at their meaning. For all we know, they might be calls of distress or courtship, which would lead to calamitous lay-by situations. More encouraging are recent experiments with Aeolian harps and sea organs—majestic instruments played by wind and water.

They fill the air with extraordinary sounds and pique the curiosity of Dragons within their considerable range. A look is as good as a landing, or at least a promising first step.

Then there is the smell of Dragons. Anyone who has spent time around enchantments knows they exude a symphony of pheromones specific to most every occasion. Depending on the season and breed, the aroma of a weyr can go from subtle hints of jade in glacial blue ice to intoxicating layers of spice mixed with sun-drenched loam and every permutation in between. Researchers working to interpret these bouquets are making inroads, but it is slow going: these are odiferous codes Johann Farina, the father of modern perfumery, would be hard pressed to decipher. At present, the best advice anyone can offer is to plant a wide variety of flowers, spices, and aromatic woods. If you enjoy walking your land, likely a Dragon will, too.

Finally, we have an approach that is a throwback to the work of Druids and wizards and is embraced by many New Agers: the mental summoning. You don't need bells and whistles or even smudge sticks (unless, of course, you like that sort of thing), just a generous heart and a strong streak of Dragon empathy. Pick a place where you feel connected to yourself and the environment, clear your mind of human clutter, engage your inner Dragon, and reach out. In your mind's eye weave a warm welcome. Visualize Dragons swooping down, if not beside you (which could be hazardous to your health), then to the most inviting part of the lay-by. Let them know you offer a safe and comfortable place where they can be themselves. Habit verging on ritual is important; to that end, send forth your psychic call at dawn and dusk—when Dragons are most active—every day for as long as it takes. And don't be greedy. By all accounts, narrower focus leads to clearer communication, so envision one or two individuals stopping in, not a whole enchantment. While credible summoners' tales speak of visitations within the first six to twelve months, doubting Thomases insist the same results have been reported where there was no outreach of any kind. Accurate though this assessment may be, it totally ignores the invaluable ripples of well-being such callings elicit. Anecdotal evidence points to happier, more affectionate Dragons and calmer, more centered people. Clearly, a little time spent communing with inner and outer Dragons is like Vitamin C—you may not be able to prove it helps, but it certainly won't hurt.

So, to summon or not to summon?

In the end, it comes down to a personal choice. The consensus in crypto sciences holds that there are currently no reliable shortcuts to enticing Dragons to your lay-by. Of course, that might change; we're learning more every day. We do know that if you build it right, they will come. It just takes time. If you have the patience, space, and inclination, jump in! You'll not only be doing a worthy deed for Dragons but also for the myriad creatures in their orbit.

In the Family

Covenant of the Dragon Keeper

I. This above all things remember:
    They are Dragons; all Dragons are wild.

II. Thou shalt love thy Dragon as thyself,
    treating her always with affection and respect.

III. Thou shalt not give thy Dragon a silly name.

IV. Thou shalt keep thy Dragon intellectually
    stimulated and physically fit.

V. Thou shalt listen to thy Dragon.

VI. Thou shalt not have fire-breathing practice near woods nor during droughts.

VII. Honor thy Dragon's Remembrance-of-Name Day and keep it holy in just Dragon style.

VIII. Thou shalt use neither saddle nor bridle on thy Dragon.

IX. Thou shalt not buzz thy neighbors' livestock.

X. Thou shalt honor thy Dragon's partnership choices and provide for her welfare after thy passing.

Dragon keeping is an ancient and honored pursuit, written records of which date back to China's Xia Dynasty (c. 2200–1600 BCE). During the reign of Shun (c. 2200 BCE), there lived a man named Tung Fu who had a remarkable fondness for and skill with Dragons. He understood their needs, their tastes (roasted swallows were a surprising Dragon delicacy), and did all he could to meet them.

Many dragons sought refuge with him and he reared the dragons according to their nature in order to serve the Emperor Shun, who gave him the surname Tung, and the family name Hwan-lung *(Dragon-rearer)* …[51]

The Hwan-lung family continued raising Dragons for generations. Anyone who had a Dragon would go to them for information, some staying on to study, a select few becoming master Dragon keepers, in time—by appointment of the emperor, of course.

---

51. Visser, *Dragon in China and Japan*, 82.

In Europe and the New World, the history of Dragon keeping is considerably less illustrious. Up until the late nineteenth century, the practitioners of record were a mere handful of Druids, wizards, and solo dracophiles. Shifts in cultural attitudes over the last hundred and fifty years have changed all that, and there are now more people interested in the care of Dragons than there are Dragons to be cared for. This is to be expected. The idea of having an intimate relationship with beings as incomparable as Dragons takes us to that magical place we've clung to since childhood. Add to that our fascination with the exotic and the dangerous— the allure of the falcon over the finch, the cobra over the colubrid—and Dragons become the *bêtes du jour*. Speak of Dragon keeping today and you are almost certainly referring to the care of Westies.

This growing popularity leads to a whole new set of problems. The fickle world of companion-creature fads combined with a rapacious free-market system makes even Dragons vulnerable to the dark side of the "animal trade." A clutch of Dragon eggs can set a poacher up for life, and latter-day dragon slayers prey on isolated enchantments, capturing orphaned hatchlings for the black market. Though better equipped to protect their own than other endangered species, Dragons—especially young ones—are not invincible. Despite being protected by canon and custom, the possibility of a huge financial windfall continues to entice mercenary individuals into Dragon territory. Under international law, should these people or any of their customers be caught by the authorities, they face six-figure fines and up to twenty-five years in prison. In recognition of the fact that these actions can destroy a whole generation of Dragons, some countries take an even harsher stance. Any repeat offender is presented with a choice: life behind bars or three weeks bare-handed in the aggrieved Dragon habitat. Survive or not, it is believed to be fair punishment, giving the guilty party more of a chance than they gave the Dragons, especially in this age of long-range, high-power weaponry.

The official position of WAFDE on these matters is to recognize the sovereignty of individual nations and weyrs and to remain as neutral as possible. To those inclined to humanize our friends, the fact that more of these offenders succumb to the elements than to Dragon wrath suggests Dragons have a more refined sense of mercy than we do. Recent studies have shown that those who make it to the other side of the experience (and a surprising number do) have a born-again admiration of and fondness for Dragons. With the zeal of the converted, many go on to devote their lives to Dragon sanctuaries and anti-poaching efforts.

Basics of Dragon Keeping

So you want to be a Dragon keeper. In theory this sounds great. The more people with hands-on understanding of the world's Dragons, the better. Knowledge breeds both respect and affection.

Of course, in practical terms, it's a different matter.

Facts are facts, and 99.7 percent of dracophiles are fundamentally unsuited to actually rearing the creatures they love. With that in mind, you must first make an honest, rigorous appraisal of your temperament and that of your immediate family. If feeding a mouse to a boa troubles your sensibilities, that's fine, but you are no Dragon keeper. If you would rather watch TV than post a property line in mid-winter, you are no Dragon keeper. And if you can't envision yourself gray-haired and liniment slathered, growing old in an enchantment's embrace, you are no Dragon keeper. Remember this: macaws are long-term, but Dragons are multi-generational. Whether you define family by blood or choice—and Dragons don't care about such distinctions—you will be entrusting their care to your children and your children's children. A full-hearted commitment from all concerned is essential.

You must also be willing to study. Some people insist that open eyes and keen intuition will cover every situation, but they're wrong. That might work for a guinea pig, but it could prove disastrous when raising an egg-covered hatchling into a well-adjusted, high-flying, fire-spitting Dragon.

That said, Lesson #1 for keepers is common sense to its core: Dragons are not pets; do not treat them as such. Treat them as equals—who breathe fire and can eat you.

For Lessons #2 through #169, check out the numerous texts of variable merit in print, bearing in mind that strict book-learning often falls short in the real world. Ideally, anyone serious about rearing Dragons should apprentice with a master keeper (WAFDE-certified, of course), much as they did in China all those centuries ago. The exchange of practical knowledge and hands-on experience are invaluable; and, for veterans, it is a way to pay it forward to a new generation. If such training is not available, the best alternative is to dive into crypto-science and zoological courses at an accredited university. Anyone who does not put in this time up front is, quite honestly, a fool. Fools and Dragon keeping do not mix. *Note: if you go the college route, be sure to check your sources and courses. Bogus classes offered by unaccredited, for-profit institutions are, in the end, worse than no education at all.*

With the character test under the bridge, you must next look at your finances. Whether providing temporary foster-age or life-long care, Dragon keeping is expensive. Habitats, food, miscellaneous extras—our friends are far from hot-house flowers, but the costs still add up. Quickly.

To begin with, you need space—at least fifty acres per Dragon.[52] On that land you must establish a proper Dragon habitat. Some of this is similar to setting up a lay-by: hunting and fishing grounds, a plethora of vegetation, a bathing area, and a fire pit. Be sure fire pits are away from the woods and houses, with access to plenty of water. (While accidents are not 100 percent avoidable, don't court them. It only raises your insurance.) The primary difference from a lay-by is in shelter requirements. For Dragons who are long-term members of the family, a simple ledge or bower will not do. They need a proper lair, natural or man-made, as big as a large barn and able to withstand anything the elements throw their way.

Half the battle in keeping a Dragon is getting her to feel safe in her abode. It is her castle—a place in which she can stretch out (or curl up), be alone or with friends (regardless of species). Décor—plants, rock formations, even a source of running water—are the personal touches that can make a simple shelter into a real home. If you foresee more than one Dragon in your life, you'll want a structure that can be

---

52. For an A to Z look at the rigors of modern Dragon keeping, see *The Dragon Keeper's Handbook*.

expanded to meet future needs. You might even consider hooking up with other Dragon keepers in a communal venture. It is a way of sharing the outlay and labor, as well as creating what amounts to an enchantment, by design if not breeding. Elders can teach Dragonlets better than the most lettered keeper, and a multi-generational environment contributes to the socialization essential for youngsters hoping to have a snowball's chance in hell of going native when they come of age. It also makes for happier Dragons. As we have seen, they are not solitary as by choice: bonds and companionship are vital to their well-being. It should be noted that some Dragons who lack the camaraderie of their own kind when very young will form unusually strong attachments with the humans in their lives and even with other animals in the family. While this is gratifying to the humans—we do so crave the affection of our companions—it can prove detrimental to the Dragons. They frequently have a much harder time making it among their own kind, often choosing to remain in the company of humans for their entire, very long, lives.

An extended community of Dragons and their people is great for keepers, too, providing the best support system imaginable. Expertise, resources, even day-to-day duties—all can be shared to mutual benefit. Community fire brigades are one of the most invaluable services such a group can offer. Not to diminish the great work done by rural and municipal fire departments, but it is a fact of life that some firefighters consider working around Dragons to be above and beyond the call. Unless you want to risk your garage going up from a stray flame on a windy day, backup plans should be made. Strength coming in numbers, a communal arrangement can also provide a little leverage with the neighbors and local authorities, in a pinch. Hopefully you won't need it, but with Dragons there are no guarantees.

Dragon Acquisition

Presuming you have the mood and means to be a Dragon keeper—and you have filled out all your paperwork and been properly credentialed—the next step is to acquire a Dragon.

There are three legal ways to get a Dragon: as an egg, an orphan, or an inheritance. We will discuss the first two here; the third, at its appropriate time.

Eggs

A Dragon egg found in the wild is as rare as an orchid in Antarctica. Should you stumble across one—or a whole clutch—chances are you're looking at a scenario in which a solitary Queen, bereft of enchantment or weyr, has been driven away from her brood or even killed. (There have been reports of lone Sires tending clutches, though these are very rare. A Sire who loses his mate is usually so grief-stricken that nesting is the last thing on his mind. He is more likely to fly off on his own for a decade or two.) That said, don't rush to judgment. A Dragon on her own cannot tend her eggs nonstop for the eighteen-month incubation period; she has to eat and drink, which necessitates leaving her eggs unattended for brief periods of time. So, if you find eggs, unless there is clear evidence of foul play or abandonment, be patient and monitor them for the next day or two. If mom doesn't return by then, contact WAFDE and take the eggs into custody.

In the absence of a Queen, it falls to the Dragon keeper to provide the two essentials of incubation: heat and song. Depending on the age of the egg, you will have to keep it between 98 and 120 degrees F. Though Dragons regulate egg temperature with remarkable precision, human efforts require thermostatically controlled nesting areas. Heating bills can be exorbitant, leading keepers to use as much solar and wind power as possible, as well as tying the nesting chamber to the rest of their estate, circulating excess BTUs to house, barn, conservatory, etc. Daily contact with the egg—talk, song, music—is essential to a Dragonlet's development, yet, because we don't tolerate extreme heat well, you must set up an air-conditioned anteroom for the comfort of non-Dragon visitors. Invite friends for reading marathons and recitals, and pipe in music at night or when you can't be there in person. A common music mistake is going all classical on your Dragons. Don't. They have been known to have eclectic tastes, enjoying most everything except elevator music. Listen for "hums" and watch for egg rocking, both indicators of happy Dragonlets.

With approximately two weeks to go before the blessed event, the shell loses its leathery quality and gets hard as stone. It is then time for hatching fire, the intense blast of flames Queen and Sire produce to give their little ones a final draconic push. Aside from strengthening the infant within, it crackles the shell so it's easier for the little one to break free. Unless you have a couple of grown Dragons on hand to help, you will need a hatching kiln—a brick dome with forced-air burners that can lick the egg with fierce but even heat. Crank it up to 2000–2200 degrees F, then cool quickly. Crackles are guaranteed. As a matter of course, hatching kilns will be egg-free most of the year. Rather than let them just sit there, many Dragon keepers have taken to using them for ceramics. If you're blessed with skill and talent, this can generate a little extra income, which is always welcome. Of course, be sure to keep the hatchlings out of your pottery unless you want to be knee-deep in shards.

Compared to hatching fire, replicating the birthing anthem is a snap—and much cheaper. Thanks to intrepid researchers at sanctuaries around the globe, keepers have access to an extensive library of natal-song recordings from over fifty distinct breeds. Even if you are not 100 percent sure if your egg holds a Cariboo Mountain snub-nose or an Athabascan Gold, chances are you'll find an anthem fit for the Dragons indigenous for your general region. Provide the sound system and ear plugs, and you're good to go. Sixty-eight hours after you take the egg out of the hatching fire, begin playing the song, starting at a whisper then rising to an ear-splitting 120 decibels. After half an hour of this, cut to silence and wait. In no time, the egg will start to roll back and forth, then, chip by chip, its occupant will use her egg tooth to crack herself free. Scrub off any shell-membrane residue, feed her immediately,[53] then celebrate. You have officially joined the ranks of Dragon keepers!

---

53. First impressions not only count but can color the entirety of a relationship. To that end, a warm (not cooked) mixture of 2 pounds ground meat, 2 pounds chopped greens, a couple of ostrich eggs, and a pound of honey makes for an excellent first meal. Consider it your initial offering, *in loco parentis.*

Orphans

A very different set of challenges face those who adopt Dragon orphans. Despite the insistance of certain individuals that only human beings (and of course their personal poodles and parakeets) have rights to feelings, anyone who has spent time among Dragons knows they have emotional lives easily as complex as our own. When a hatchling is orphaned, chances are they lost not only their parents but also one or more siblings or weyr mates. To say their trauma and subsequent grief will be profound is an understatement. For this reason, the keeper who takes in an orphan needs to be as much a shrink as a zoologist.

The most common problems you'll deal with are refusing to eat, depression, and hostility towards people—or, the reverse, intense separation anxiety. Don't delude yourself: there are no quick fixes to any of these issues. Empathy goes a long way—putting yourself in their place—as does the company of other Dragons, if possible. In cases of depressed appetite, hand-feeding is a must, and mostly greens for the first week (it's easier to get down than animal proteins). Also, spicing their food with extra ginger or cayenne pepper can spur their salivary glands into action. Be sure to drop a vitamin/mineral supplement in, too. Young Dragons grow so fast that missing even a couple of meals can send them down the road to malnutrition. In extreme cases—and only with orphans over six months old—keepers have been known to mix an ounce of medicinal cannabis (marijuana) into the feed. It is enough to promote the munchies without serious intoxication or adverse side effects.

Weyrsickness remedy, a staple in every Dragon keeper's medicine chest, can help take the edge off depression. A powerful drug made from bittersweet, honey, and forget-me-nots, it's the standard treatment for post-hatching blues but must never be used for long-term or chronic conditions. The best thing for a melancholy Dragon is to distract her. Spend lots of time with your little one and keep her occupied. Go for walks together, play games, groom her daily from tip to tail. Let her know you care for her, love her, and are not going to leave her alone.

Hostility problems are, obviously, the trickiest orphan issue to handle. You're dealing with creatures who have experienced the worst our species has to offer, and until we can regain their trust, they will react to us with natural fear and anger. This is not only stressful for a Dragonlet, but potentially very dangerous for us. It goes without saying that patience and gentility are crucial. Be sure your Dragon has plenty of room and a retreat which she knows is a Dragon Only area. Provide the best of hatchling cuisine, talk to her when you can, but keep your distance. Work and play, be yourself. If you have pets, interact with them where she can watch; if you have other Dragons (or can invite someone with Dragons over), even better. With luck, she will soon realize that you are not like the other two-legs she's encountered in her young life.

Then you can begin the next phase: getting her used to you in her environment and, ultimately, to your touch. Be careful: there are apt to be setbacks, just don't let them cost you a finger. At the first sign of her emotional pendulum swinging too far in the other direction, turning her into a one-person Dragon, have her spend quality time with others in your circle, both human and animal. If problems persist, do not hesitate to seek professional help. Keep your local WAFDE chapter on speed dial and an excellent

Dragon vet/therapist, too. (Some would add their local EMTs and a good plastic surgeon to the list. Accidents happen.) An overly protective hatchling can become an uncontrollable adult. No matter what, your keeper's pride should never get in the way of doing what is right for your Dragon, up to and including relocation for her or you.

In the end, the rule for an orphan is simple: Watch and listen; be compassionate, loving, and steady. You are her family now—the only one she's got—and you're stepping into some very large footprints. It will take time for you both to make the adjustment.

How to Talk to Dragons

A few words are due regarding communicating with Dragons. History tells us of a rare handful of people—sorcerers and shamans with solid backgrounds in both belief and linguistics—who were positively fluent in Dragonese. They could sit for hours and converse with the enchantments, learning the secrets of the cosmos, the treasures and pitfalls of their shared environments, not to mention magical wonders beyond human imagining. Of course, history is written by those who can write, so exaggeration is not out of the question. One thing is certain: much has been lost through the ages of human history, including the knowledge of how to talk to Dragons.

Thankfully, efforts are being made to turn that around. Cryptolinguists have been working for years compiling an elementary lexicon of Dragon-speak, but it is proving a mind-bending project. Nuances of tone and volume, let alone the idiomatic nature of the language, put the task of making Dragonese accessible on a par with cracking Mayan hieroglyphs. The experience has taught us that while Dragons have a great facility for understanding human speech, modern keepers and dracophiles are far less adept with *lingua draconia*. Indeed, for all our talk about the superiority of human intelligence, it is curious to note that not only Dragons, but dolphins and even rats and dogs understand our words far better than we'll ever understand theirs.

The absence of a common language does not mean the absence of communication. Dragons have highly developed intuitive and telepathic abilities, not to mention being masters of body language, from the twitch of a tail to the slightest nostril flare. Posture, head bobs, wings sleeked back or full-sail—all these have very specific meanings. Some of this is breed specific, so you must pay close attention. A spade droop from a traditionally restrained Bi-Polar Equator Jumper, for example, indicates a deep blue—almost navy—mood. From a more gleeful Lapland Lacewing, though, it simply signals the desire to play. Nasal flares are an almost universal warning sign except during mating season, when romance is literally in the pheromone-laden air and unattached Dragons are on the alert. Curiously, baring fangs (usually in conjunction with a deep-throated growl), while an obvious "back off" signal from Westies, is a sign of greeting among Oriental Dragons.

There are a few cross-breed body-language basics. Standing stiff-legged with neck frills unfurled always means, "This is my space and I will defend it with my life!" That Dragon is obviously feeling stressed and must be given a wide berth. On the other hand, a Queen with an open brow, gently snuffling her hatchlings' faces and rubbing their neck scales is in serious maternal mode, offering affection and care. If she offers the same to you, rejoice! You have been accepted as one of her own, the highest honor a Dragon can bestow. The list goes on and is being constantly extended thanks to the rigorous work of keepers around the world.

Daunting as the prospect of talking with Dragons might seem, know that you are not alone in your endeavor. Dragons in the company of people display a genuine desire to communicate, and in this—as in most things—they will gladly meet us halfway. A keeper remotely attuned to the mystical should have little trouble establishing a basic rapport with their little one. Approach the task with an open mind; use simple words, enunciate clearly, and remember that eyes have the power to speak volumes. Atop a good foundation, anything is possible.

Growing into Dragonhood

Now is the time to settle into being with and raising your Dragon. During the first few years as substitute parent, you must teach her survival skills: hunting, fishing, what and how to forage. Whenever possible, enlist the aid of other Dragons. No matter how experienced and dedicated you are, there will always be certain things better taught by her own kind. Be firm but caring—especially with matters of safety. A Dragon who does not understand proper boundaries is a risk to herself and everyone around her. If your goal is to release your charge back into the wild, you will want to instill in her a healthy wariness of humans. This can be a delicate balancing act: ten to fifteen years in fosterage cannot help but create a level of attachment on both sides.

Watch out for boredom. Young Dragons are like any other children: full of energy and inclined to get into absolutely everything. This curiosity, while it makes them very receptive to training—as much as you can ever train a Dragon—will definitely keep you on your toes.

A regimen of nutrition and exercise is very important to a growing Dragon. Once weaned away from ostrich-egg-based pap and onto solid fare, their diet should include 50–55 percent animal proteins (heavy on the fish and fowl, light on red meat), 40 percent vegetables, and 5–10 percent minerals. Calcium and Vitamins C and D are particularly important during the first few years, when growth is fast and furious. Dragons, like guinea pigs, are unable to synthesize Vitamin C, so it must be a daily component of their food. Peppers (hot and bell), dark greens, and a host of fruits all meet this need and provide enough diversity to please most tastes. In the beginning, hunting skills will naturally be more miss than hit, so be sure to monitor their weight and supplement as needed. That said, it's important for young Dragons to be self-sufficient and not rely on you for meals they should be catching themselves. Aside from that, variety is important: Dragons are great experimenters and will sample most anything in the process of educating their palate.

Play and hunting lessons take care of the essentials of physical fitness, and they're good for you, too. When youngsters turn three and prepare to take wing, they will need to build up their flight muscles. This is something they manage quite well on their own, though a little encouragement never goes amiss. A good bath and grooming after exercise wards against muscle stiffness and provides an excellent opportunity for bonding.

Names

Naming is an issue that's plagued Dragon keepers for years. Between two and four years of age, every Dragon experiences what is aptly known as the Remembrance of Names. It is best explained as a time when Dragonlets tap deep into their species/familial past and draw forth the name with which they were born. There is no guarantee they will tell you, of course—Dragons know the power in names and will not share theirs with just anyone. Keepers who are conscientious and loving stand a good chance of being let in on the secret. Until then, though, if you are inclined to hang a handle on your youngster, do so knowing it's a temporary convenience at best. Stay away from anything cute—cute is not appreciated. Call a Dragon Huggy-Buns Crash-Bandicoot and the wrath of Tiamat will rain upon you with a vengeance! Generally, variations on "Dragon" are acceptable, though don't let that be an excuse to check your creativity at the door. Linguists that they are, Dragons enjoy the touch of the exotic, a hint of far off places. To that end, we offer the sounds of the word *Dragon* from around the world:

Albanian: Dragua

Athebaskan: Manchu

Basque: Erensuge

Breton: Dragão

Bulgarian: Drakon

Chinese: Lung/Long

Croatian: Zmaj; Azdaja

Dansk: Drage

Dutch: Draak

English:
    Old: Draca
    Middle: Dragun
    Modern: Dragon

Esperanto: Drako

Estonian: Lohemadu/Tuuleus ("Wind Snake")

Finnish: Lohikäärme/Draakki

Gaelic: Arach

Germanic: der Drache

Greek: Drakos

Hawaiian: Kelekona

Hebrew: Drakon

Hungarian: Sárkány

Icelandic: Dreki

Indonesian/Sanskrit: Naga

Japanese: Ryu

Norse: Ormr

Polish: Smok

Portuguese: Dragão

Romanian: Balaur

Russian: Drakon

Slovenian: Zmaj

Thai: Mung-Korn

Tibetan: Brug

Turkish: Ejderha

Vietnamese: Con rông

Welsh: Ddraig

Zulu: Uzekamanzi

Pick something fun, something with a lilt that makes your young one prick up her ears and sit tall!

Fire and Flight

Now, charge ahead and make memories. Every Dragon and their keeper are unique, and, as such, hold different memories near and dear. That said, fire and flight are regulars on most top-ten lists. Fire is all flash and fury and a true test of whether or not your Dragon takes you seriously. Of course, flaming comes to them during their terrible twos when *high-spirited* and *rebellious* are watchwords of the day. If you have taught her well, she'll know where and when fire is allowed: away from house and woods, only when accompanied by you or an elder Dragon you can trust, and never during a drought. An isolated sand or gravel pit is perfect for little ones just getting the hang of their fiery abilities. You should also have plenty of water on hand in case of a mishap. Maturity and practice lead to control and accuracy, qualities upon which you should insist before letting your Dragon employ flame and flight together. Thankfully, you'll have a year to get her ready for that.

Dragons on the wing are a sight to steal your breath. The possibility of flying with them, perched astride scaled muscle, the beat of wings matching the beat of the heart, is the stuff our dreams are made of. It is only natural, then, that first flight is anticipated by Dragon and Dragon keeper alike. For little ones, it is a rite of passage—the final step on their way to Dragonhood. Within a month of turning three, a Dragon's "baby" wings shed their velvet flocking and sprout into great leathery sails, big enough and strong enough to keep her aloft. In the wild, this is an occasion for group grooming and establishing ties, many of which lead to lifelong pairings. In the absence of other Dragons, keepers are proxy weyr mates, helping to burnish budding wings clean and smooth. Beyond grooming and cheering loudly in support, there is little a human can do. Catching the wind beneath her wings is what a Dragon is designed for. From the most tentative glide to elaborate aerobatics, inside of a year a Dragon will be navigating the skies with the grace of a seasoned pro.

Under rare circumstances when a fledgling is having trouble getting aloft, Dragon keepers have been known to use Flying Ointment, an herbal extract of foxglove, windflower, mugwort, and basil oil (Witches' Herb). This highly concentrated (and volatile) fluid is diluted and sprayed on a young Dragon's wings. Powerful brew or well meaning placebo, keepers have sworn by Flying Ointment for years. (See *The Dragon Keeper's Handbook*, page 243, for precise instructions on preparation and use.)

By her fifth year, a Dragon should have matured enough to carry a person. Not that all Dragons will. Some, even the most affectionate, simply refuse to be ridden. Don't take it personally, it's just their way. For those who don't mind riders, there are a few hard and fast guidelines:

1. No tack. Bridles, saddles, even saddle pads—all are draconic taboos. Wedge yourself between the dorsal ridges just ahead of their wings and grip with your knees—hard.

2. Follow all laws and courtesies of the skies, including observing no-fly zones and not spooking neighbors' herds. This is for everyone's safety and promotes the image of Dragons as socially acceptable beings eager to play along, even by others' rules.

3. Before traveling abroad, check with WAFDE and the appropriate consulates; have all necessary documents in order. Borders may be irrelevant at 1,500 feet, but international incidents over forgotten licenses or missing visa stamps are no fun for anyone.

Aside from that, dress warm, hang tight, and have fun! "In dreams," Madeleine L'Engle wrote in *Walking on Water*, "we are able to fly … and that is a remembering of how we were meant to be." Flying with Dragons is the promise of those dreams made real.

Maturity and Later Years

The tough part of Dragon keeping is basically over by a Dragon's sixth year. Wise in the ways of hunting and munching, named, fired up, and on the wing, they are nearly as large as an African elephant and can embrace their top-predator status with glee. As they continue their steady march to maturity, parasites and illness become all but distant memories. True, accidents can happen, but the sturdiness of Dragons makes a vet generally unnecessary. (Do keep a blacksmith on call. They are as good as vets—sometimes better—for tooth and claw care or should a horn get chipped and need attention above and beyond basic charming.)

The biggest worry for a keeper comes when the curious frivolity of youth topples headlong into unpredictable adolescence. Hormones and pheromones kick in and even the best-behaved Dragons are apt to act up/act out. If you've left chinks in their upbringing, they will find them. This means reinforcing rules and remaining vigilant. Idleness leads to trouble, so activity is the natural antidote and perfect opportunity to impress upon your charge a sense of being part of the larger community. Urge her to chip in with challenges and chores that stretch both mind and body; if you can work in conjunction with your local municipalities, so much the better. Dragons get a kick out of earthworks of any kind, from shaping parks and playgrounds to raising flood walls and clearing fire breaks (which is far less ironic than it sounds). They are also keen to help with search-and-rescue efforts, their fierce senses and mobility making them invaluable in times of natural disaster. Eager as Dragons are to lend a paw, bear in mind that they are neither pets nor beasts of burden. Always ask, never command. Such deference goes a long way, particularly with adolescents.

Returning to the Wild

If you have been rearing your Dragon with an eye to returning her back to the wild, years ten through fifteen are periods of evaluation and choice. Be clear-eyed and unsentimental. Look at your Dragon not as the hatchling or orphan you've shepherded into young adulthood, but as a creature on the verge of independence—if she's ready and willing, that is. The finest care and intentions in the world cannot make for a successful release should a Dragon choose not to go. Conversely, some people hope for a life-long commitment only to find their twelve-year-old companion is craving open skies and new horizons. In the end, all you can do is raise her to be the best Dragon she can be and honor her decision. Be cheered by the fact that Dragon memories are as long as their lives: even after years with a wild weyr, they may return to visit the place they called home and the people they called family in their formative years. They may even surprise you by having a whole new generation of Dragonlets in tow.

Speaking of that next generation, the mating game is something all Dragons face in time, even those who remain in the company of people. Whether for breeding or affection, partnership preferences crystallize long before Dragons reach sexual maturity. Depending on the breed, females become sexually mature between thirty-five and fifty years old; add an extra decade to that for males.

Since the solitary life appeals to only about a third of all Dragons, keepers must be prepared for major changes. When the time comes, you will either have to bring another Dragon into your fold or work out a joint arrangement with the keeper of the chosen mate. Hopefully, they will be in your vicinity (another reason to cultivate a solid keepers' network), though long-distance relationships are not unheard of. The details may take a little negotiating, but if it makes everyone happy—and perhaps brings a clutch or two into the world—it's well worth it.

Travel and Festivals

In and around these monumental lifestyle choices, you and your Dragon will have years in which to learn how to be with each other and how to be apart, how to work, and—most importantly—how to have fun. Joseph Campbell wrote, "Nobility of spirit is the grace—or ability—to play, whether in heaven or on earth."[54] And Dragons love to play; the sky is literally the limit when it comes to draconic recreation. Travel is a pastime tailored to their curiosity and adventurousness. It's also well within the means of most keepers, especially those who enjoy roughing it. You won't even need a tent: a Dragon wing makes an excellent lean-to. Just pack a sleeping bag and your papers and you can explore the world.

Doing the festival circuit can be a real treat and a half. Originating in an age when our friends shimmered with the divine, Dragon Festivals of yore were a means of showing reverence, asking for aid, and having a rip-snorting good time all in one glorious afternoon. While the religious aspects have largely fallen by the wayside, hundreds of revelers still gather from the Pacific Rim to Great Britain to celebrate with races, dancing, and Dragons in the streets.

For water lovers—and all of our companions qualify—Dragon-boat festivals are universal fun. They began thousands of years ago in China as a lunar celebration held on the fifth day of the fifth lunar month—rice-planting time

---

54. Campbell, *The Masks of God*, Vol. 1, 27.

around the Summer Solstice. The festivities were designed, some insist, as a way to get into the Dragon King's good graces and ensure a bountiful harvest. They were rough and tumble events, rumored to include drowning sacrifices and crews assaulting one another with stones and bamboo flails. Considerably tamer Dragon-boat races crossed the ocean to Vancouver, British Columbia, for the 1986 World's Fair. An instant success, the races' popularity spread across Canada, to Europe, and beyond. Today, Dragon regattas are held in seventy-four countries. Though sport has replaced religion, they remain an exuberant testament to the affection with which Dragons are regarded around the world.[55]

Land-based celebrations abound, too, though their flavor tends to be more localized, centering on Dragons—often pseudo-dragons—out of regional legend rather than the species as a whole (not that others aren't welcome). In Europe many of these fetes started out as victory laps for the local hero who bested a fierce brute and saved a grateful populace. Now they showcase the more pro-Dragon sentiments of the world and welcome well-behaved Dragons of all kinds. You can go to Provence, France, for example, where St. Martha is celebrated for taming the tarasque, a most unpleasant first-century creature with a taste for peasants and priests. Draconic figures are paraded through the street and pyrotechnics illuminate the night sky.

If you and your Dragon are more old-school, you can go to the British Isles. In February, the city of Norwich turns

---

55. Check with the International Dragon Boat Federation (www.idbf.org) for a full schedule of events. If you time it right, you can travel around the globe from March to December, hitting one event after another.

into Dragon Central for two full weeks. You can frolic with Dragons and dracophiles from around the globe, join in on the grand procession, even tap your toes with Morris dancers in a joyful tradition that dates back to medieval Guild times. From there, take a leisurely trek along St. Michael's ley line, one of the most powerful Pagan paths in Great Britain. A veritable Dragon carriageway, it runs from nearby Lowestoft through the Chiltern Hills to Glastonbury then on to St. Michael's Mount and Land's End. Take side trips to Stonehenge for Summer Solstice, then hop across the Bristol Channel to Newcastle Emlyn, Wales, for the Heart of the Dragon Festival in early July, for a grand adventure! According to legend, long, long ago, the last Dragon in Wales died near Newcastle Emlyn. Lamenting the loss as any good Welsh village would, the citizens were naturally overjoyed when a Dragon egg was found, nurtured, and hatched. Celebrating the return of the *Ddraig* is the core of the Heart of the Dragon Festival. While the veracity of this claim is moot—as the thriving enchantments of Anglesey and the Cambrians will attest—never let facts get in the way of a good legend or a good party.

For New World Dragons with a taste for the desert and a decidedly American experience, attending Burning Man is a must on the annual agenda. Burning Man is held in the Black Rock Desert, a few hours north of Reno, Nevada. There, for a week from the end of August through Labor Day, a temporary community of thousands springs up. With a focus on self-reliance, self-expression, and an absolute respect for the environment, the festival embraces the beliefs and attitudes of Dragons and their people, and welcomes any and all who wish to participate. In addition to such a warm reception, the desert locale means you don't have to worry about space—easily a thousand Dragons and keepers can make camp without fear of crashing into someone else's abode. The flaming of the Burning Man is, understandably, a highlight of the event, but Dragons are equally drawn to the strict adherence to "leave no trace behind." Indeed, many Dragons and their people gladly stay on after the fact, lending a paw to the Earth Guardians and Bureau of Land Management agents in the land's restoration. (See www.burningman.com for more information.)

Legend and lore are not the only inspiration for such celebrations. In recent years, the growing number of sanctuaries and lay-bys has led to a surge in Dragon fetes as a way for neighboring peoples to celebrate the beings they've come to know and love. Whatever their origin, they promise good times for all.

When the seasons turn cold and flight courts more frostbite than usual, Dragons (except polar breeds who are used to extreme conditions) gladly stay at home and hunker down in their dens. Lest they get fidgety or pack on unwanted hundredweights, you should set up a routine that balances work and games, with the emphasis, of course, on the games. Favorites include King of the Hill, Air Soccer, and Hide the Bauble (great fun around Yule time and birthdays as it makes the giving of presents an interactive event).

Old Age

Father Time, Charles Dickens remarked in *Barnaby Rudge*, "tarries for none of his children," not even Dragons. Yet Dragons who choose a life among people do so with the understanding that *lifetime* is not an absolute concept. They'll be a good fifty years shy of their prime when we're fighting the exhausting onslaught of old age, a reality that necessitates far-sighted, posthumous planning. Have all your legal ducks in a row, including a designated Dragon-keeping heir. Before signing and sealing anything, be sure to talk these things through with all the parties involved. While it may be a pleasant surprise to find you've inherited Grandma's cameo, a Dragon can't be tucked into a jewelry box and taken out only for special occasions. It is usually best to keep such arrangements in the family, but if that is not possible, anyone can be a viable candidate as long as they are knowledgeable and Dragon-approved. Of course, self-determination is a draconic hallmark, and no matter what plans we may make, some of our friends will be die-hard one-person Dragons. Such creatures may stick around through the will-reading as a matter of courtesy, but then they're gone with a whoosh and nary a word.

As mentioned in chapter 1, Dragons untouched by knight or natural disaster are not immortal. Though details on longevity are still sketchy at best, cryptogerontologists—experts in draconic golden years—put life spans between 250 and 400 years, depending on species and breed. This means that, somewhere along the meandering stream of time, a Dragon will have their last Dragon keeper. If you are that person, there are a few things you should know. First, Dragons are not like people. They don't show their advancing age until they are positively ancient. In human terms it's like looking and feeling thirty until you hit eighty-five. Suddenly—over a couple of years—their scales will lose their luster, their claws and horns become fragile. Appetites will be less robust than usual as they spend more time in the sun than hunting and leave energetic games to the great-great-great-granddragons.

As a keeper, turn your empathy on high and be attentive to your Dragon's needs. Provide her favorite food and drink, file down broken horns, and hook up extra UV lamps and heaters in her den—the cold can affect senior Dragons down to their bones and make them snappish.

No one knows exactly what happens when a Dragon's allotted time runs out. Reports are that they're here one day, then simply gone the next. But where? Poets speak of the Kingdom of the Eternal Dragon and it is as likely a destination as any other. For those left behind, there is the unavoidable burden of loss. Hold tight to the moments you shared together, the years spent in incomparable fellowship, lest regret sours you on giving time and affection to future generations. Tell stories, but with joy instead of tears. And in the deep night, when grief taps your shoulder unawares, look up to the sky you danced across so often and remember the wisdom of the Inuit:

Perhaps they are not stars, but rather openings in heaven where the love of our lost ones pours through and shines down upon us to let us know they are happy.

epilogue

Pondering the Unthinkable: A World Without Dragons

Myth, metaphor, and magnificent flesh—in the once-upon-a-time of human history, we've watched Dragons from afar and pulled them close as skin. In the process we nearly drove them over extinction's precipice, only to catch our breath and draw back in the nick of time. But what if we had succeeded? What would our world—our lives—be like without Dragons?

No Dragons? Never, you say! While most dracophiles would agree with you, the very fact we can put the possibility into words must give us pause. Painful though the idea is, it would be remiss of us not to take the long view and ponder the unthinkable. Worse yet, imagine a Capraesque *It's A Wonderful Life* nightmare in which Dragons had never been born. Oh, what a barren dystopia we would live in if the skies did not crackle with Dragonfire, the air not ripple with Dragonsong. The repercussions run long and deep, demanding that we look at what we are willing to give up. What parts of our heritage, our futures, our very selves are we willing to live without?

From a strictly naturalistic point of view, despite naysayers and know-nothings, Dragons are barometers *par excellence* of Earth's health. Any wilderness that can't support Dragons has long since been unable to support the rest of us. Indeed, this fact convinces many that, given our relative frailties, Dragons will outlast us by eons. Cryptoherpetologists hope they are right—who better to inherit Earth than Dragons! But such hopes do not take into account the vulnerability of numerous lesser species, some of whom are literally hanging on by a thread. Far too many species have vanished in just the last fifty years—some without even being known—for us to be nonchalant about a Dragonless world. We must remain mindful that, while we have been playing dice with our habitat, we have no right to do the same with theirs (or any other species'). Casual observers have suggested that Dragons will simply do as they did before when things got bad: retreat beyond the mystic veil until our senses and the planet recover. This is a comforting notion, yet it neatly avoids all those inconvenient truths about our responsibility for driving them away in the first place. As we frack our Earth and turn the oceans and rivers into toxic wastelands, we spin the facts and convince ourselves it's not our fault. Rather than heed how Dragons live in balance with the planet, our race toward global devastation only accelerates. After all, Dragons can survive most anything.

But the question then is: why should they have to? It is the ultimate test of our covenant to remember that, like the rest of us, Dragons need and deserve a tolerable planet to live on, and then work to make it so. If we fail and Dragons leave us for realms otherworldly or unknown, we will have gone far beyond the province of environmental protection. We will have cut to the quick our inner selves, excising with spoon, not scalpel, the enchantment we carry within, the wonder that informs our dreams. For Dragons are as eternal as the land and stars; larger and fiercer than we could ever hope to be.

They're monstrous, too, but that's as they should be. We need monsters. They are the fearful challenges we face and strive to overcome on our way to becoming complete human beings. By confronting real monsters, we confront the subtler, more sinister shades lurking within our subconscious. And what creature is more equal to the task than a Dragon? As complex and perceptive as we are, in their monster state they are our wild counterpart. They soar through our psychic skies without ties to civilization or religion, without the burden of good or evil, virtue or sin. They are Dragons in Eden before the Fall and, standing talon to toe, teach us, even today, that our inner monsters are not half as bad as we think.

As the world shifted from primitive black and white to draconic Technicolor, respect and honor replaced our fear and loathing. We looked to the vaulting heavens and knew there was no one else we could summon to light the dark, to fill us with majesty when the universe made us feel small. In a sign of our shifting spirituality, we opened our eyes, beholding Dragons less as we imagined them and more as they are: totems of justice, wisdom, magic, and what William James referred to as the "ineffability" of the mystical. They aren't saints by any means, but in an age when science pushes us to explain everything, their wordless wonder is a precious tonic for the soul. We walked with them, flew with them, and they blessed us with their loyalty and willfulness. Their awesome splendor. They have been generous with their teaching, giving us the strength and the courage to believe in the rare and unusual. Most of all, they have been patient, even when we did not deserve it. Now, rather than shun them, we can claim our inner Dragons with a discerning wink and prideful roar!

How can we lose even one bit of all that is Dragon without betraying them and every other species on the planet? More on point, how can we make sure we never do?

Today we say we embrace Dragons in their infinite diversity. It fills us with politically correct thrills and self-less warm-fuzzies; yet talk is cheap, and even the most PC appearances can be deceiving. If history teaches us anything, it is that there will always be virulently anti-Dragon factions with slings, arrows, and howitzers at the ready. With small minds—and even smaller spirits—they are latter-day Dark-Timers, still insisting Dragons are evils standing against progress, profit, and morality. They're pushing Dragons, trying to make them push back, to retrofit them into old-fashioned monsters more easily feared, more eagerly fought. If these foes had their way, they would diminish Dragons until they become invisible, once and for all.

Less overt—yet ultimately more dangerous—are the multitudes of people walking through their lives with little belief in anything beyond their own noses. But the fact that they do not interact with Dragons—or even see them— does not mean their lives don't impact the enchantments in real and devastating ways. Just because you've never seen a blue-horned tzeltal doesn't make you blameless of their deaths when you clear-cut their rain forest. Of course, such individuals hardly miss what they never knew was there. Their flagrant disregard for the world around them leads to the sort of head-blindness that denies climate change and overpopulation or sees no purpose in protecting species or safeguarding the purity of our air and water.

In the face of such hostility and willful ignorance, preventing a Dragon doomsday scenario, farfetched as it might seem, is paramount. True, a century of shifting human perceptions (not to mention serious groveling) has led to real progress between our species. But it's not enough. We must not let current pro-Dragon choruses turn to funeral dirges. In the fights to come—and they will come—we must stand with Dragons as they stood with us.

As we walk—and fly—through the world, we must move with the grace of diplomats. We are ambassadors for Dragon/ human alliances. We must honor myth and lore but support Dragon Studies at every turn, lest superstition and outright lies overshadow facts and empirical knowledge. Wherever we find them, we must seek to open eyes and nurture the smallest sparks of belief in truths beyond everyday comprehension, buoyed by the fact that the wonder with which Dragons infuse the world is a big tent. With no help from us, it sheds "enough light for those who want to believe and enough shadow to blind those who don't."[56] And that is as it should be.

---

56. Blaise Pascal. *Pensées*. 1669.

As you leave Dragon Country, remember this: In the end, the fight for Dragons is a fight for ourselves, and it is our very need that keeps them with us. From the smallest house dragon to the grandest emerald Queen, Dragons are the sinew that binds us to Earth, to the mystical, and to each other. They are the joy and truth—the inspiration, even—of the universe. We hold on to them, we thrive; we let them go, we die.

It is simple. Without their glory and grandeur, their supernal nobility lifting our eyes, we would still be struggling to see beyond the next hill, not looking to the stars. For humanity to survive,

> *it is not light that is needed, but fire; it is not the gentle shower, but thunder. We need the storm, the whirlwind, and the earthquake.*[57]

We need Dragons.

---

57. Frederick Douglass. "What to the Slave is the Fourth of July." Corinthian Hall, Rochester, NY. 1852.

glossary

Adopt-A-Dragon (AAD) Program: Project started by the Dragon Conservancy Program modeled after the U.S. Bureau of Land Management's National Wild Horse and Burro Program and the American Bear Association's Friend of the Cubs. It is a way Dragon lovers around the globe can, for a modest fee, stay connected to these marvelous creatures and feel like they are contributing to the continuance of Dragon welfare the world over. http://mackenziesdragonsnest.com/adopt adragon.html

Aido Hwedo: The Great Rainbow Serpent of the Fon people of Africa who was both aide and friend to the Creator, Mawu. After the world was made, Aido Hwedo wrapped her coils tightly round it to hold it together until the end of time.

Alkha: Cosmic Dragon from the tales of Siberia's Buriat people, so massive his wings covered the heavens. Occasionally he would nibble on the sun and the moon but would throw them up again when their heat became too much for him to stomach. Lunar craters are said to be Alkha's tooth marks.

amphiptere: A winged, legless pseudo-dragon similar in appearance to the French guivre. Ill-tempered and much feared, the creature's image was often used on warriors' shields to frighten the enemy.

Apophis: The moon Dragon of ancient Egypt who lurked in the Nile, waiting to swallow the sun god Ra at the end of the day. Fortunately, Ra didn't taste good, and Apophis would spit him out so that the sun might rise anew.

aspis: Very dangerous European pseudo-dragon, whose bite and touch are said to be fatal. It is susceptible to the entrancing force of music, so much so that aspises are known to stick their tail in one ear and place the other to the ground. This contorted posture allows their victims to escape with relative ease. If you find a dead aspis, do not touch; even in death, they can be lethal.

Baba Yaga: Supernatural character from Russian folklore who is everything from a witch to a wise Crone, depending on her mood and who you talk to. She was known to consort with Dragons, especially Koschei, the Deathless One.

beithirs: A thick-tailed, wingless pseudo-dragon found in the Scottish Highlands. They are very dangerous and should be approached with extreme caution (or left alone).

Cadmus: Greek dragon slayer, Dragons-teeth sower, and founder of Thebes. The Dragon Cadmus slew was sacred to Ares, which ticked the god of war off no end. After years of servitude and torment, in an act of truly karmic proportions, Cadmus, believing the gods favored Dragons over people, chose to end his life as a Dragon.

Campacti: Cosmic Dragon of Mexico from whose body the Earth was made.

cenotes: Water-filled sinkholes found in the Yucatan and environs. They were often sacred to the indigenous peoples of the area and treasured as bathing/watering spots for local Feathered Dragons.

charming: The act of burnishing horns. A common grooming ritual for Dragons and Unicorns.

Cintamani: The divine wish-granting pearl from the Hindu and Buddhist traditions of Asia. It is thought by some to be the pearl sported by Asian Dragons and is equated to the alchemist's Philosopher's Stone.

cornicles: Small horns found on a Dragon's blaze. Unlike a Dragon's large horns, cornicles are believed to be largely ornamental. Not that they can't inflict injury—any Dragon horn can—but that's not their primary function. (To the best of our knowledge.)

crepuscular: Active at dawn and dusk, like most Dragons.

crypto sciences: Crypto = hidden or secret. The crypto sciences are studies of all things not readily apparent to the casual observer. Some people believe the subject creatures are complete fabrications; the crypto scientist believes they are simply hidden. When it comes to Dragons, pertinent branches of the crypto sciences include:

Crypto-anthropology: The study of the impact fabulous creatures have on human culture. Some crypto-anthropologists are tipping the field on its head and looking at the social structure within a particular clan of creature. This is particularly germane to Dragons given the tight-knit nature of their society.

Cryptoherpetology: aka Secret Serpent Science, Remarkable Reptile Research, and Dragon Studies. *The* field for serious dracophiles. Cryptoherpetology also covers such non-dragons as the cockatrice, chimera, and a wide variety of water beings who fall in that gray area between fish and reptile.

Cryptogerontology: The study of aging in Dragons.

Cryptomythology: The study of sifting through what is real and what is myth in human lore, oral history, and ancient epic.

Cryptopaleontology: Fossil science as it relates to the exploration of the world of hidden beings. When it comes to Dragons, the lack of fossil record has frustrated cryptopaleontologists greatly.

Cryptoveterinary: The medical branch of the crypto sciences. Crypto vets look at diseases and treatments for mundane ailments which may cross over to the mystical as well as those specific to our friends in the crypto kingdom. Dragons, being by and large hale and hardy, tend to have little use for cryptoveterinary aid.

Cryptozoology: The umbrella field of study for all creatures strange and unusual, from abadas to zlatorogs. And, naturally, Dragons.

Dark Times: A particularly rough period in Western Dragon history when our friends were under attack on all sides. It lasted roughly from the rise of Western monotheism until the Late Middle Ages (c. 1500 CE). The Dark Times were not humanity at its best.

diggers: A class of pseudo-dragons who, as their name suggests, burrow beneath the ground. They were often tracked and hunted for their ability to find rich mineral deposits treasured more by us than them.

dracophile: A Dragon lover. Like you.

Dragon Conservancy Program: Modern movement dedicated to preserving Dragons and Dragon habitat for the present and future. The Dragon Conservancy is behind the Adopt-A-Dragon initiative, among other efforts. http://mackenziesdragonsnest.com/dragonconservancy.html

Dragon lay-by: A Dragon-friendly patch of land established for the rest and recreation of itinerant Dragons.

Dragon sanctuaries: Internationally recognized safe havens surrounding every known wild weyr in the world. Dragon sanctuaries are essential for keeping wild Dragons safe and sound.

dragon slayers: Their numbers are, woefully, legion. Some were canonized: George, Margaret, Michael, etc. Some were given hero's laurels and royal crowns: Gilgamesh, Rustam, Hercules. For our purposes, the less said about them, the better.

Dragon Studies: See *Cryptoherpetology*.

drakes/draks/drachs: Heavy set, wingless pseudo-dragons. In the past, drakes were frequently beset by dragon slayers and their deaths counted in the anti-Dragon tally.

Druids: Ancient sages and mystics of Europe. The Druids were instrumental in keeping Dragons in the world.

Edda (Poetic* and *Prose): Icelandic masterpieces from the thirteenth century CE and attributed to Snorri Sturluson. They speak at length of the Twilight of the Gods and the role the Miðgard Dragon plays therein.

enchantment: The basic draconic family unit or clan. A modern enchantment includes from 10–15 individuals.

endo-, ecto-, and kleptothermic: Terms referring to how organisms regulate their temperature. Endotherms are warm-blooded, ectotherms are cold-blooded, and kleptotherms borrow (steal?) heat from others. Dragons are all of these things and more. See *gigantotherm*.

Epirotes: Maternal Dragon Apollo placed in charge of rearing Python's children at what was, essentially, the first Dragon sanctuary of record.

Eurynome: Primal Mother of ancient Pelasgian cosmology. She created—then married—the great Dragon, Ophion, and from their union created all things in the universe.

flying ointment: A medicinal concoction for Dragons who are having a little trouble getting aloft. It can be very unstable and must be handled with the greatest care.

Fu-Ts'ang: Dragon of Hidden Treasures. The epitome of the hoarding Dragon, Fu Ts'ang protects and rules all ores and precious stones under the Earth.

Gandareva: Cosmic Dragon from Sumer who stretched from the ocean floor to the starry firmament. For all his ferocious ways, Gandareva kept an even more dangerous Dragon in check. Unfortunately, he was slain by Keresaspa and the second Dragon was free to destroy the universe.

gargoyles: Tenacious pseudo-dragons from France. They were used by aristocrats and vintners as watchdragons with mixed—and messy—results and were all but eradicated during the Reign of Terror (1793–94).

gigantotherm: Any creature, like the largest dinosaurs and, of course, Dragons, massive enough to maintain a constant, active, body temperature even though they are not strictly speaking warm-blooded.

Gilgamesh: Babylonian hero-king and dragon slayer who merited a tale of his own, *The Epic of Gilgamesh*. Among his string of "heroic" deeds, he killed a Dragon guarding a tree sacred to the goddess Inanna.

Gondwana: Vast supercontinent which broke into Africa and South America (c. 130 million years ago), resulting in the transatlantic spread of Feathered Dragons.

gowrow: New World pseudo-dragon found in the Ozarks and surrounding wilderness. Their habitat has been seriously threatened by recent human sprawl in Arkansas and Missouri.

guivre: Lake dragon from France. Seldom seen today, though quite numerous during the Middle Ages, guivres are frequently confused with amphipteres.

house dragons: A class of small pseudo-dragons who, if treated well, will protect your home, guard your valuables—especially children—and even increase your wealth. The latter can be at your neighbors' expense, which can lead to unanticipated incivility and local feuds. Common house dragons include Scandinavian husorme; Welsh fferm gwybers; the pisuhänds, smij, naui, and aitvaras of Eastern Europe; the gnar (house), mandir (temple), and dhuan (smoke) nagas of India— not to be confused with the less-sociable jungle nagas; and the tangaroas of the Pacific Islands.

hydra: A multi-headed water pseudo-dragon indigenous to Mediterranean lands. The most famous hydra is the Lernaean Hydra, offspring of Echidna and victim of Hercules's labors.

iaculus: A tree-skimmer pseudo-dragon from Africa. They are protectors of tombs and mediators between the living and dead. Known as the javelin snake, they will hurl themselves at anyone trespassing on their territory.

Keresaspa: Quasi-divine dragon-slaying hero from Sumer. See *Gandareva*.

Kids For Dragons (KFD): An offshoot of the Adopt-A-Dragon initiative geared at budding dracophiles (sixth grade and up). By working in conjunction with schools around the world, KFD brings kids and young Dragons together and offers wonderful opportunities for field trips.

Koschei: Mean-spirited Dragon cohort of Baba Yaga. He was known as the Deathless One because his soul was separated from his body and hidden far, far away. Only by uniting body and soul could a hero hope to slay him.

Kurgan civilizations: Ancient peoples who moved from Central Asia into Europe bringing their Dragons with them.

Ladon: Wise Dragon of ancient Greece. The son of Echidna, Ladon lived in the garden of the Hesperides where he guarded Hera's golden apples. He spoke fluent Greek and was very content until, fulfilling his eleventh labor, Hercules killed him and stole the apples.

lake dragons: A vast class of pseudo-dragons found around the globe. They come in all shapes, temperaments, and sizes. Champ in Vermont, Ogopogo in British Columbia, and the Misiganabic of Quebec are examples of notorious lake dragons.

ley lines: aka Dragon Currents or e[nergy]-lines. The electromagnetic grid which crisscrosses the planet. Dragons are very sensitive to ley lines and will take up residence on or near a ley line nexus whenever possible.

Marduk: God of Ancient Babylon and slayer of the Cosmic Dragon, Tiamat.

marsh draks: Pseudo-dragons known for their outsized appetites and carelessness with fire. Unrestrained marsh draks have driven numerous wetland species to the brink of extinction, as well as setting peat bogs on a slow burn.

Mawu: Androgynous Creator of the Fon universe. A very Dragon-friendly individual. See *Aido Hwedo.*

megafauna: The huge land creatures of post-dinosaur Earth, including mammoths, indricotheres, giant sloths, cave bears, and Dragons. Today megafauna are few and far between and include elephants, rhinoceros, and, of course, Dragons.

Miðgard: The middle realm—the Earth—of the Norse cosmos.

Miðgarðsormr: Cosmic Dragon of the Norse people. The unruly son of Loki, as a Dragonlet, Miðgarðsormr was hurled into the ocean that surrounds the Earth. With the Twilight of the Gods, he hauls himself up onto the Earth and partakes in its destruction until slain by Thor.

monitors: Family of large lizards including Komodo dragons and the fast, whippy-tailed Perenties of the Australian outback.

Muchalinda/Mucalinda: Benevolent naga who sheltered Gautama beneath his hood as a torrential storm raged about them.

Nazca lines: Mysterious geoglyphs in Peru's Nazca Desert. Local Dragons are known to use them as guides for their flying workouts.

Niðhögger: Cosmic Dragon of the Norse who is wrapped round Yggdrasil, the World Tree, constantly nibbling away at its roots, working towards the destruction of the world.

Ophion: Cosmic Dragon created by Eurynome. A bit of a braggart, a trait which, ultimately, led to his downfall.

Otherworld: Celtic realm of the dead, the faërie (*sidhe*), and other deities and spirits. It is believed the *sidhe* welcomed beleaguered Dragons into the Otherworld to weather the worst of the Dark Times.

ouroboros: Pseudo-dragon frequently depicted holding his tail in his mouth. The ouroboros is symbolic of the eternal circle of life.

pax loci: "Peace of the Place." The rule that governs all Dragon lay-bys and guarantees a civil stay for all who drop by.

peiste: A large water pseudo-dragon from Ireland. Though it was suggested that St. Patrick drove them out of the Emerald Isle, recent sightings suggest otherwise.

Permian and Cretaceous Extinctions: The most devastating extinction-level events the planet has experienced. Occuring 250 million years ago, the Permian Extinction wiped out 90 percent of all marine life and 70 percent of all land vertebrates. The Cretaceous Extinction of 65.5 million years ago saw the end of almost 80 percent of all species. Dragons (proto-Dragons) managed to survive both.

piernas cuelebre: A rare eight-legged pseudo-dragon indigenous to the Pyrenees Mountains.

Popol Vuh: The sacred book of Maya cosmology. It speaks extensively of the various Feathered Dragons—Sovereign Plumed Serpent, Vision Serpent, et al.—central to the Mayan faith.

pre-Raphaelites: Nineteenth-century school of artists, writers, and aesthetes. Their dedication to Renaissance ideals and their interest in ancient Celtic and Arthurian legends helped revive the interest in the Druids and, consequently, in Dragons. The Pre-Raphaelite Brotherhood included Dante Gabriel Rossetti, John Millais, Edward Burne-Jones, and William Morris.

proto-Dragons: The very first hardly-recognizable-as-Dragons Dragons who walked the earth, swam the seas, and filled the skies at the start of draconic evolution.

pseudo-dragons: A broad class of creatures who, in the popular imagination, are frequently lumped together with True Dragons but who are distant relatives at best. The ranks of pseudo-dragons include wyverns, nagas, house dragons, wyrms, and drakes, to name but a very few.

pterosaur: "Winged lizards." Flying reptiles who filled the skies from the late Triassic to the late Cretaceous periods (220–65 million years ago). Due to their leathery wings, it was erroneously believed for many years that pterosaurs were the direct ancestors of Dragons. Though they were contemporaneous with early Dragons they are most definitely not related.

pyronic sacs: Fire sacs. Anatomical structure essential to the production of Dragonfire. Pyronic sacs are vestigial at birth and only develop fully as a Dragon enters her second year.

Python: The prophetic Dragon of Delphi. Apollo slew her and buried her beneath the Delphic temple that her oracular powers might transfer to the women who served in her stead. In her honor, the Delphic oracles were called the Pythia.

Queen: A breeding female Dragon.

Quetzalcoatl: The Cosmic Feathered Serpent (Dragon) of Mesoamerica.

Ragnarök: The End of Days in Norse mythology. It is the time when the destroyer Dragons Miðgarðsormr and Niðhögger break their bonds and wreak havoc upon the worlds of men and gods.

Rahab: An Old Testament Dragon mentioned in Psalms. He was bested by Yahweh.

Rainbow Serpents: Cosmic Dragons who travel the Dream-time and serve as right hands to the Creators. Aido Hwedo, Minia, and Degei are but a few Rainbow Serpents who have helped shape the world. In Australia, the Rainbow Serpent is one of the most powerful totemic figures of the Aboriginal peoples.

Remembrance of Names: Solemn event in the life of every True Dragon when they, quite literally, remember their name. This usually happens in a Dragon's third year, though some youngsters are more precocious than others. For Dragon keepers and their Dragons, it is a time of great celebration.

ropen: Small, bipedal pseudo-dragon from the rain forests of Papua New Guinea. The ropen can be easily mistaken for a large fruit bat but is actually one of the last descendants of ancient pterosaur/proto-Dragon hybrids from the Triassic Period.

Rustam: Hero and dragon slayer from ancient Zabulistan.

ryu-jin: Generic water dragon spirits in Japan. They're very important to the island nation, which depends so extensively on water for health and livelihood.

Ryu-jin: The Dragon King who lives in the sea off the coast of Japan. His daughter fell for a human and their descendants became the imperial line of Japan.

Saints Petroc and Carantoc: A brace of medieval Welsh saints who, when challenged to remove pesky Dragons, were wise enough to approach the tasks with words and faith rather than swords. Their approach may be indicative of the long-standing Welsh affinity for Dragons.

Shen Lung: The spiritual Dragon who rules the rains of China. The Emperor alone could display his likeness.

Sire: A breeding male Dragon.

Sovereign Plumed Serpent: aka Gucumatz. The Cosmic Feathered Dragon of Maya cosmology (see *Popol Vuh*). Gucumatz joined with Heart of Sky and brought the world into being. It took them several tries, but eventually they got it right. With creative duties behind him, Gucumatz transformed. See *Vision Serpent*.

Tanakh: The Hebrew Canon.

Tiamat: Cosmic Dragon of the ancient Near East. Tiamat was Chaos personified. Her downfall led to the Creation of the World and the dawn of civilization.

Trans-Atlantic Transmigration: An exodus of a passel of adventurous European Dragons who were fed up with the rampant anti-Dragon sentiments coursing through Britain and the Continent in the Dark Ages. Shortly after the Saxon invasion of the British Isles, they heeded the call to "Go west, young Dragons!" and crossed the Atlantic. In the New World they made their way among the enchantments of North America.

tree-skimmers: An arboreal class of pseudo-dragons who soar and glide through the jungles, real and concrete. In the wake of lost forest habitat, some have adapted to the glass-and-steel of metropolitan areas. They can be found by observant dracophiles hanging out on skyscraper ledges and in the company of cathedral gargoyles.

True Dragons: The three species of big-*D* Dragons: Western or European Dragons, Eastern or Asian Dragons, and Feathered or Southern Dragons. All others are pseudo-dragons. Accept no substitutions.

tyr druics: Cornish earth dragons—diggers—who can be found in abandoned tin mines and sauntering across Bodmin Moor beneath the full moon.

Vision Serpent: A transformation of Sovereign Plumed Serpent, he is the Cosmic Feathered Dragon who perches atop the Mesoamerican foliate World Tree. He brought civilization to the people and was invoked as a war god when necessary.

Vritra: Three-headed Vedic Chaos Dragon. Vritra drank the waters of the world dry, only disgorging them when defeated by Indra and his thunderbolt.

weyr: A Dragon community. In the old days, a weyr could easily accommodate five to seven enchantments. Unfortunately, everything is down-sized today: modern weyrs are two to three enchantments large at most.

Weyrsickness: aka Dragon Despondence. An ailment of the spirit which can afflict Dragonlets just out of the egg, especially those who are orphaned or abandoned. The best course of treatment is time, affection, and liberal doses of Weyrsickness Remedy.

World Association for Dragons Everywhere (WAFDE): A global organization whose sole purpose is to preserve and protect the world's Dragons. WAFDE serves as a resource center for Dragon keepers and dracophiles, is charged with inspecting and licensing Dragon lay-bys, and works with various mundane conservation organizations to put an end to poaching of Dragons and the more familiar creatures integral to their ecosystems. http://mackenziesdragonsnest.com/WAFDE.html

wyrms: Massive, legless pseudo-dragons frequently found in underground caverns, wells, and old mines.

wyverns: One of the most recognizable of the pseudo-dragons, the wyvern has wings but only hind legs. Much smaller that True Dragons, wyverns frequently bore the brunt of Dragon-hunting zeal and were mistaken for True Dragons by artists no less than Leonardo da Vinci, Raphael, and Paolo Uccello.

Yggdrasil: The World Tree in Norse cosmology. The Dragon Niðhögger is coiled around its roots, noshing away as the spirit moves him, until such time as he gnaws them through, heralding the Twilight of the Gods and the world's end.

Zu: Cosmic Dragon from ancient Mesopotamia. Zu was the consort of Tiamat and sire of her wild, unruly brood.

bibliography

Books

Agrippa, Henry Cornelius. *Three Books of Occult Philosophy.* Translated by James Freake. St. Paul: Llewellyn Publications, 1993.

Bently, Peter, ed. *The Dictionary of World Myth.* New York: Facts on File, Inc. 1995.

Beowulf: The Harvard Classics, Vol. 49. Translated by Francis B. Gummere. New York: P. F. Collier & Son, 1910.

Bettelheim, Bruno. *The Uses of Enchantment: The Meaning and Importance of Fairy Tales.* New York: Random House, Inc., 1977.

Bissell-Thomas, J. *The Dragon Green.* London: Robert Hale Ltd., 1936.

Campbell, Joseph. *The Flight of the Wild Gander.* New York: Harper Perennial, 1990.

———. *The Masks of God, Vol. I-IV.* New York: Viking Penguin, 1977.

———. *Transformations of Myth Through Time.* New York: Harper & Row, 1990.

Conway, D. J. *Magical Mystical Creatures.* St. Paul: Llewellyn Publications, 2001.

Cunningham, Scott. *Encyclopedia of Magical Herbs.* St. Paul: Llewellyn Publications, 1996.

da Vinci, Leonardo. *The Notebooks of Leonardo da Vinci.* New York: Reynal & Hitchcock, 1939.

Frazer, Sir James G. *The Golden Bough, Abridged: Vol. 1.* New York: Macmillan Co., 1922.

de Groot, J. J. M. *The Religion of the Chinese.* New York: Macmillan Company, 1910.

I Ching, The. Translated by Richard Wilhelm and Cary F. Baynes. Princeton, NJ: Princeton University Press, 1967.

Ingersoll, Ernest. *Dragons and Dragon Lore.* Mineola, NY: Dover, 2005.

Johnsgard, Paul, and Karin Johnsgard. *A Natural History of Dragons and Unicorns.* New York: St. Martin's Press, 1982.

Kakuzo, Okakura. *The Awakening of Japan.* New York: The Century Company, 1905.

——. *The Book of Tea*. New York: Dover Publications, 1964.

Krishnamurti, Jiddu. *Beginnings of Learning*. New York: Harper & Row, 1975.

Kynes, Sandra. *Whispers from the Woods: The Lore & Magic of Trees*. Woodbury, MN: Llewellyn Publications, 2006.

Lao-Tzu, and Jonathan Star. *Tao Te Ching: The Definitive Edition*. New York: Jeremy P. Tarcher/Putnam, 2001.

Lao-Tzu, and Ursula K. Le Guin. *Tao Te Ching: A Book About the Way and the Power of the Way*. Boston: Shambhala Press, 1997.

Le Guin, Ursula K. *Earthsea Trilogy: A Wizard of Earthsea, The Tombs of Atuan, and The Farthest Shore*. New York: Bantam Books, 1977.

——. *The Farthest Shore*. New York: Bantam Books, 1972.

L'Engle, Madeleine. *Walking on Water*. New York: North Point Press, 1995.

Lewis, C. S. *The Chronicles of Narnia*. New York: Collier Books, Macmillan Co., 1972.

——. *The Discarded Image: An Introduction to Medieval and Renaissance Literature*. Cambridge: Cambridge University Press, 2009.

MacKenzie, Shawn. *The Dragon Keeper's Handbook*. Woodbury, MN: Llewellyn Publications, 2011.

Malory, Sir Thomas. *Le Morte d'Arthur*. New York: New American Library, 1962.

Matthews, John, and Caitlin Matthews. *The Element Encyclopedia of Magical Creatures.* London: Harper Element, 2005.

McCaffrey, Anne. *A Diversity of Dragons.* New York: HarperCollins, 1997.

———. *Dragonsdawn.* New York: Del Rey, 1989.

———. *The Dragon Riders of Pern.* New York: Del Rey, 1988.

Popol Vuh. Translated by Dennis Tedlock. New York: Touchstone Books, 1996.

Prince, J. H. *Languages of the Animal World.* Nashville, TN: Thomas Nelson Inc., Publishers, 1975.

Rilke, Rainer Maria. *Letters to a Young Poet.* New York: W. W. Norton & Co., Inc., 1962.

Robinson, James M., ed. *The Nag Hammadi Library in English.* New York: Harper & Row, 1988.

Rose, Carol. *Giants, Monsters & Dragons: An Encyclopedia of Folklore, Legend, and Myth.* New York: W. W. Norton & Co., 2000.

Scamander, Newt. *Fantastic Beasts & Where to Find Them.* New York: Scholastic, 2001.

Schele, Linda, and David Freidel. *A Forest of Kings: The Untold Story of the Ancient Maya.* New York: William Morrow & Co., 1990.

Schele, Linda, and Peter Mathews. *The Code of Kings: Language of the Seven Sacred Maya Temples & Tombs.* New York: Scribner, 1998.

Schele, Linda, David Freidel, and Joy Parker. *Maya Cosmos: Three Thousand Years on the Shaman's Path*. New York: William Morrow & Co., 1993.

Simpson, Jacqueline. *British Dragons*. Ware, Hertfordshire, UK: Wordsworth Editions Limited, 2001.

Spenser, Edmund. *The Faerie Queene*. London: Penguin Classics, 1979.

Tolkien, J. R. R. *The Hobbit*. New York: Ballantine Books, 1970.

———. *The Lord of the Rings*. New York: Houghton Mifflin, 1994.

de Visser, M. W. *The Dragon in China and Japan*. Amsterdam: Johannes Muller, 1913.

Young, Dudley. *Origins of the Sacred*. New York: St. Martin's Press, 1991.

Internet References

Accessed June 2012

Aprocrypha, The. "Bel and the Dragon." Internet Sacred Texts Archive. www.sacredtexts.com/bib/apo/bel001.htm#001.

Beckett, Samuel. "Worstward Ho." The Samuel Beckett On-Line Resources. www.samuel-beckett.net/w_ho.htm.

Curry, Andrew. "Gobekli Tepe: The World's First Temple?" Smithsonian.com. www.smithsonian.com/history-archaeology/gobekli-tepe.html.

King, L. W. "The Seven Tablets of Creation, Enuma Elish." Internet Sacred Texts Archive,www.sacred-texts.com/ane/stc/index.htm.

Kúnos, Ignácz. "Forty-four Turkish Fairy Tales: The Black Dragon and the Red Dragon." Internet Sacred Texts Archive. www.sacred-texts.com/asia/ftft/ftft41.htm/.

Lang, Andrew, ed. "The Yellow Fairy Book." Project Gutenberg. www.gutenberg.org/files/640/640-h/index.htm.

Parkinson, Danny J. "British Dragon Gazetteer." *Mysterious Britain & Ireland*. www.mysteriousbritain.co.uk/england/legends/british-dragon-gazetteer.html.

Spalding, Tom. "Dragons in Art and on the Web." 2000–2005. www.isidore-of-seville.com/dragons.

Tolkein, J. R. R. "On Fairy-Stories." http://brainstorm-services.com/wcu-2004/fairystories-tolkien.pdf.

recommended reading

Allan, Tony. *The Mythic Bestiary: The Illustrated Guide to the World's Most Fantastic Creatures.* London: Duncan Baird, 2008.

Ashman, Malcolm. *Fabulous Beasts.* Woodstock, NY: Overlook Press, 1997.

Blanpied, Pamela Wharton. *Dragons: The Modern Infestation.* Woodbridge, Suffolk, UK: Boydell Press, 1997.

Calasso, Roberto. *Ka: Stories of the Mind and Gods of India.* New York: Vintage, 1999.

———. *The Marriage of Cadmus and Harmony.* New York: Alfred A. Knopf, Inc., 1993.

Campbell, Joseph, and Bill Moyers. *The Power of Myth.* New York: Doubleday, 1988.

Clark, Jerome. *Unexplained.* Detroit: Visible Ink, 1999.

Conway, D. J. *Mystical Dragon Magic.* Woodbury, MN: Llewellyn Publications, 2009.

Dann, Jack, and Gardner Dozois, eds. *The Dragon Book.* New York: Ace Books, 2009.

Dickinson, Peter. *The Flight of Dragons.* New York: Harper & Row, 1979.

"Dragon Dreaming." http://dragondreaming.wordpress.com.

Drake, Ernest. *Dragonology.* Somerville, MA: Candlewick, 2003.

Ellis, Peter Berresford. *The Druids.* Grand Rapids, MI: Wm. B. Eerdmans Publishing Co., 1994.

Enchanted World: Dragons, The. Alexandria, VA: Time Life Books, 1984.

Grant, John, and Bob Eggleton. *Dragonhenge.* London: Paper Tiger, 2002.

Graves, Robert. *The White Goddess.* New York: Noonday Press; Farrar, Straus & Giroux, 1975.

Greer, John Michael. *Monsters.* St. Paul: Llewellyn Publications, 2001.

Mabinogion, The. Translated by Jeffrey Gantz. New York: Penguin, 1976.

Mack, Carol K., and Dinah Mack. *A Field Guide to Demons, Fairies, Fallen Angels and Other Subversive Spirits.* New York: Henry Holt & Co., 1998.

Maybury-Lewis, David. *Millennium: Tribal Wisdom and the Modern World.* New York: Viking, 1992.

Pratchett, Terry. *Guards! Guards!.* New York: Harper/HarperCollins, 2008.

William-Ellis, Amabel. *Fairy Tales from the British Isles.* London: Blackie & Son, Ltd., 1962.

Wrede, Patricia. *The Enchanted Forest Chronicles: Dealing With Dragons/Searching For Dragons...* New York: Scholastic, Inc., 1993.

Yeats, William Butler. *Mythologies.* New York: Macmillan, 1969.

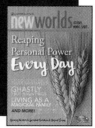

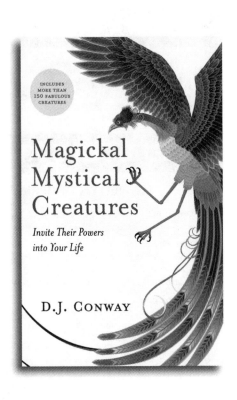

INCLUDES
MORE THAN
150 FABULOUS
CREATURES

Magickal
Mystical
Creatures

*Invite Their Powers
into Your Life*

D.J. CONWAY

Magickal, Mystical Creatures
Invite Their Powers into Your Life
D.J. CONWAY

Unicorns, centaurs, gorgons, and gargoyles . . . Enlist the special energies of over 200 fabulous creatures and mythical beasts on the astral plane to empower your magickal workings, rituals, and potential for success. Call upon a Magical Serpent for that financial windfall, or let the Phoenix help you resurrect your hope and energy!

978-0-7387-5742-1, 272 pp., 6 x 9 **$17.99**

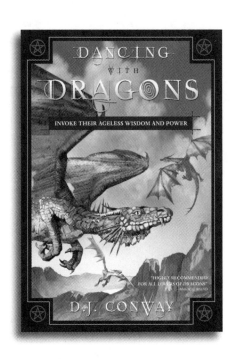

DANCING WITH DRAGONS

INVOKE THEIR AGELESS WISDOM AND POWER

"HIGHLY RECOMMENDED
FOR ALL LOVERS OF DRAGONS"
—MAGICAL BLEND

D.J. CONWAY

Dancing with Dragons
Invoke Their Ageless Wisdom and Power
D. J. CONWAY

As magickal allies or guardians, dragons can help you solve everyday problems, protect your home, and grow spiritually. Exploring the fascinating history of dragons in legend and mythology, this unique book will help you understand these ancient, powerful creatures that thrive on the astral plane. Conway describes many different kinds of dragons and explains how they are magickally linked to the elements and the planets. Through spells and rituals, you'll discover how to contact dragons, befriend them, draw on their power, and channel dragon energy.

978-1-56718-165-4, 320 pp., 7 x 10   **$21.99**

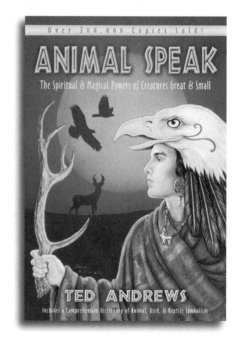

ANIMAL SPEAK

The Spiritual & Magical Powers of Creatures Great & Small

TED ANDREWS

Includes a Comprehensive Dictionary of Animal, Bird, & Reptile Symbolism

Animal Speak
The Spiritual & Magical Powers of Creatures Great & Small
TED ANDREWS

The animal world has much to teach us. Some animals are experts at survival and adaptation, some never get cancer, and some embody strength and courage, while others exude playfulness. Animals remind us of the potential we can unfold, but before we can learn from them, we must first be able to speak with them.

In this book, myth and fact are combined in a manner that will teach you how to speak and understand the language of the animals in your life. *Animal Speak* helps you meet and work with animals as totems and spirits—by learning the language of their behaviors within the physical world. It provides techniques for reading signs and omens in nature so you can open yourself to higher perceptions and even prophecy. It reveals the hidden, mythical, and realistic roles of 45 animals, 60 birds, 8 insects, and 6 reptiles.

Animals will become a part of you, revealing to you the majesty and divine in all life. They will restore your childlike wonder of the world and strengthen your belief in magic, dreams, and possibilities.

978-0-87542-028-8, 400 pp., 7 x 10   **$22.99**

To order, call 1-877-NEW-WRLD
Prices subject to change without notice
Order at Llewellyn.com 24 hours a day, 7 days a week!

An Everyday
Guide to Their
Spiritual Songs
& Symbolism

The
Healing Wisdom
of BIRDS

LESLEY MORRISON

The Healing Wisdom of Birds
An Everyday Guide to Their Spiritual Songs & Symbolism
Lesley Morrison

As spiritual guides, otherworldly allies, and magical companions, birds have been revered for millennia. This comprehensive collection of bird spirituality explores the rich beliefs and practices surrounding the winged ones—and how these venerated creatures can guide us today.

Drawing on mythology and traditions of worldwide shamanic cultures—from modern times to the Bronze Age—Lesley Morrison examines avian spirituality from all angles: what birds have symbolized through the ages and why; bird deities from Aphrodite to the Hindu goddess Saraswati; their presence in ancient cave art, shapeshifting rituals, magic practices, and religion; and the unique relationship birds share with shamans and other magical people.

From the five stages of soul alchemy to finding your bird totem, *The Healing Wisdom of Birds* offers practical ways to connect with these sacred creatures.

978-0-7387-1882-8, 240 pp., 5³⁄₁₆ x 8   **$16.99**

KONSTANTINOS

VAMPIRES

THE

OCCULT

TRUTH

Author of "Gothic Grimoire" & "Nocturnal Witchcraft"

Vampires
The Occult Truth
KONSTANTINOS

Tales of mysterious blood drinkers and life-stealing phantoms have fascinated and terrified people from all over the world for centuries. What is the truth behind the legends of the undead?

For the first time ever, here is convincing evidence that vampires really exist—and that the actual truth about vampires is stranger than anything you may have read, heard or dreamed about! *Vampires: The Occult Truth* contains first-hand accounts of encounters with vampires and vampirism of all types—the ancient undead of folklore, contemporary mortal blood drinkers who believe themselves to be vampires, and the most dangerous of all: psychic vampires who intentionally drain the life force from their victims.

Vampires is the first book to consider vampires from an occultist's point of view, and to present solid esoteric theories to explain their existence. You'll read case histories of real modern and historical contacts with vampires and victims of vampirism—including those personally encountered by the author himself—and you'll learn a simple yet powerful technique that will protect you from attacks by psychic vampires. Uncover the occult truth about an ancient legend who's still prowling the streets today!

978-1-56718-380-1, 208 pp., 6 x 9   **$16.99**

KONSTANTINOS

Werewolves

The Occult Truth

Werewolves
The Occult Truth
Konstantinos

How does one become—or kill—a werewolf? Where do our modern shapeshifting stories come from? Are werewolves real? The truth is much stranger than fiction.

Werewolves investigates the centuries-old myths and compelling evidence surrounding these enigmatic beasts of literary fame. Explore four types of werewolves—involuntary, voluntary, other-dimensional beings, and astral—plus Native American beliefs, ancient legends from cultures worldwide, true stories of sightings, and scientific theories. From shamanistic practices and curses to drug-induced hallucinations and serial-killer werewolves, this book will tantalize readers.

Also includes authentic rituals for werewolf transformation!

978-0-7387-2160-6, 216 pp., 6 x 9   **$16.95**